A Treatise on the

Alteration of Money

Sources in Early Modern Economics, Ethics, and Law

General Editors

Jordan J. Ballor, Acton Institute
Stephen J. Grabill, Acton Institute

The disciplines of economics, ethics, and law cannot be detached from a historical background that was, it is increasingly recognized, religious in nature. Economists Adam Smith and Léon Walras drew on the work of sixteenth- and seventeenth-century Spanish theologians who strove to understand the process of exchange and trade in order to better articulate subjective value, a dynamic theory of money, the role of the merchant, and the concept of marginal utility. Likewise, political theorists John Neville Figgis and Otto von Gierke drew on the work of sixteenth- and seventeenth-century Dutch, Swiss, German, and Spanish jurists and ethicists who articulated concepts that laid the foundation for federalist political structures, constitutionalism, popular sovereignty, natural-law jurisprudence, and limited government in the Western legal tradition. After a long period in which economics, ethics, and law became detached from theology, many economists, legal scholars, political theorists, and theologians now see the benefit of studying early modern economic, ethical, and legal texts in their full cultural, often religious, contexts. This series, Sources in Early Modern Economics, Ethics, and Law, provides first-ever English translations and editions of some of the most formative but previously inaccessible texts that shaped the disciplines of economics, ethics, and law in the early modern era and beyond. These inexpensive translations of seminal texts will make substantive contributions to contemporary interdisciplinary discussion.

EDITORIAL BOARD

A TREATISE ON THE

Alteration of Money

Juan de Mariana

Translated by Patrick T. Brannan
Annotations by Stephen J. Grabill
Introduction by Alejandro A. Chafuen

CLP Academic

GRAND RAPIDS · MICHIGAN

Refo500

A Treatise on the Alteration of Money

© 2011 by Acton Institute

Translated by Patrick T. Brannan

Cover image: Toledo Skyline Panorama, Spain, December 2006
Source: David Iliff, licensed under the Creative Commons
Attribution 3.0 Unported license
URL: http://creativecommons.org/licenses/by/3.0/

ISBN 10: 1-880595-88-5
ISBN 13: 978-1-880595-88-6

British Library Cataloguing in Publication Information Available

Library of Congress Cataloging-in-Publication Data

Juan de Mariana (1536–1624)
    A Treatise on the Alteration of Money / Mariana, Juan de

CHRISTIAN'S LIBRARY PRESS
  An imprint of the Acton Institute
  for the Study of Religion & Liberty
161 Ottawa Avenue, NW, Suite 301
Grand Rapids, Michigan 49503
Phone: 616.454.3080
Fax: 616.454.9454
www.clpress.com

Copy edited by Jan M. Ortiz
Interior composition by Judy Schafer
Cover design by Peter Ho
Editorial assistance by Dylan Pahman

Printed in the United States of America

CONTENTS

Sources in Early Modern
Economics, Ethics, and Law

Series Introduction

Jordan J. Ballor
Stephen J. Grabill

For the same underlying reasons that moral theology is held in disrepute by many Western intellectuals, modern economists tend to glibly dismiss or even simply ignore the economic ideas of the scholastics, whether those of the twelfth or the seventeenth century. For many intellectuals nowadays, moral theology has come to signify a passé form of religious thinking that embraces irrationality and dogmatism, and economic historians—along with notable astrophysicists, geneticists, paleontologists, political analysts, philosophers, and ethicists—have all espoused this line of thought. Among the latter, in particular, the identification of scholastic economics (or the "canonical concept of market behavior," as it is sometimes called) with Aristotelian metaphysics and ecclesiastical authority has made modern economic professionals reticent or, at the very least unreceptive, to acknowledging any sophisticated analytical contribution to monetary and value theory by the Schoolmen or the Doctors—their sixteenth- and seventeenth-century heirs.

The severing of economic ideas from their original historical and metaphysical contexts becomes especially pronounced in the contemporary debate over the prehistory of economics. Invariably, most mainstream economic historians locate the birth of modern economics in Adam Smith, the mercantilists, and the physiocrats. For historian of economics Mark Blaug, the prehistory of economics begins with the seventeenth-century mercantilists and not, as the revisionists insist, with either the ancient Greeks or the medieval scholastics. He coins the term *pre-Adamite economics* to methodologically define and restrict the era of prehistory to Smith's immediate and direct historical precursors: the seventeenth-century mercantilists, the physiocrats, and the British free-trade writers of the eighteenth century.

The broader question of whether the prehistory of economics should start in the thirteenth century or much earlier is, in Blaug's estimation, "an afterthought."[1] An afterthought, we might infer, which could presumably surface information that would challenge positivist assumptions about human behavior and social cohesion and one that will yield few, if any, new insights into quantitative methods and models. Where the scholastics analyzed economic and commercial transactions as either ethical or legal matters involving the application of natural law to civil contracts, "it was the mercantilists," contends Blaug, "who, long before Adam Smith, broke with the canonical conception of market behavior as a moral problem and fashioned the concept of 'economic man.'" These mercantilists

> believed in the direct power of self-interest and in matters of domestic economic policy came near to advocating laissez-faire. Adam Smith was not the first to have confidence in the workings of the 'invisible hand.' Nor is it necessary to appeal to scholastic influences to account for his grasp of the determination of prices by demand and supply.[2]

---

1. Mark Blaug, *Economic Theory in Retrospect*, 5th ed. (Cambridge: Cambridge University Press, 1997), 29.

2. Blaug, *Economic Theory in Retrospect*, 31.

Regardless of whether it is necessary to appeal to scholastic influences to explain how Smith, in particular, understood price and value to be determined, such a determination does not speak to the wider issue of whether such seminal figures in the history of economics as Bernardo Davanzati (1529–1606), Hugo Grotius (1583–1645), Samuel von Pufendorf (1632–1694), Gershom Carmichael (1672–1729), Francis Hutcheson (1694–1746), Jean-Jacques Burlamaqui (1694–1748), Adam Ferguson (1723–1816), Ferdinando Galiani (1728–1787), Auguste Walras (1801–1866), and Léon Walras (1834–1910) were influenced by scholastic treatments of price and value. Neither does this judgment determine, for that matter, whether Smith's entire system of thought remains intelligible if the role he assigns to teleology, final causes, divine design, and virtue is disregarded as merely ornamental.[3] In this wider respect, therefore, the modern quibble over scholastic influences in Smith is a red herring because, as Langholm attests, it sidesteps serious historical investigation into the continuities and discontinuities between scholastic and modern economic ideas.[4] Furthermore, it also has the convenient side effect of

---

3. See James E. Alvey, "The Secret, Natural Theological Foundation of Adam Smith's Work," *Journal of Markets & Morality* 7, no. 2 (Fall 2004): 335–61. See also Paul Oslington, ed., *Adam Smith as Theologian* (New York: Routledge, 2011).

4. "From an analytical and terminological point of view," writes Langholm, "there is much of scholastic teaching that can be seen to have survived into modern economics. This is not surprising, since (at least if this observation is limited to our Western civilization) it was in the high Middle Ages that the foundations were laid for the kind of systematic reasoning about social relationships that has run on continually to the present day. Sometimes, as in the case of the fairness of the market price, it was deemed pertinent above to point out a subtle shift in the moral basis that supported an apparently unaltered doctrine. Elsewhere, where doctrines have changed as radically as in the case of lending at interest, the scholastics can still be credited with posing the terms of an ongoing argument. Therefore, it would seem that much of the old vessel remained to receive new content. The question is how completely it was ever emptied of the

downplaying the importance of teleology and natural theology in the thought of Smith himself and other seventeenth-, eighteenth-, and nineteenth-century political economists.

By methodologically constricting the prehistory of economics to the mercantilists and the physiocrats, as positivist historiographers commend, economic history congeals around such characteristically "modern" concerns as the concept of "economic man," self-interest, and the emancipation of economics from the so-called canonical concept of market behavior. This arbitrary limitation of which ideas and which people carry weight in economic history only serves to bolster twentieth-century positivist assumptions, particularly those of value neutrality and *homo economicus*, the assumption that humans act as rational and self-interested agents who desire wealth, avoid unnecessary labor, and seek to order their decision making exclusively around those goals. In the end, the modern reduction of the prehistory of economics to the seventeenth-century mercantilists can be put in the form of an Occam's razor-like question: Why appeal to scholastic influences to illumine modern notions of money, value, and price when all the basic elements of classical economics are already embedded in mercantilism?

The most straightforward reply is that seminal ideas, which include revolutionary economic ideas, never develop in intel-

---

ferment prepared for it in the medieval schools. This subject requires a book rather than a few lines. In fact, it has been the subject of many books, some of them provoked or inspired by Max Weber's ideas about religion and capitalism. For simplicity, let us recall that scholastic economics rested on three intellectual traditions. The first support was the tradition of the Bible and the Church Fathers with its emphasis on individual duty. The second was the tradition of the recently rediscovered Roman law with its emphasis on individual rights. The two traditions were made to balance briefly and precariously in the Thomist synthesis by means of a third support in Aristotelian social philosophy." See Odd Langholm, "Scholastic Economics," in *Pre-Classical Economic Thought: From the Greeks to the Scottish Enlightenment*, ed. S. Todd Lowry (Boston/Dordrecht/Lancaster: Kluwer Academic Publishers, 1987), 132–33.

lectual, historical, religious, philosophical, or geographical vacuums. "Enlightened," secular reaction to the medieval Church's temporal jurisdiction and to theology's intellectual hegemony as the queen of the sciences has created a modern milieu in which scholars are no longer even aware of the historical influence that fundamental Christian doctrines have exerted in Western culture and university life.[5] From very early times, Christian theologians assumed that the application of patterns of discursive reasoning (as in the scholastic method, which was a method instituted by medieval Christian theologians and adapted and applied for subsequent centuries) could yield an increasingly accurate understanding not only of God's word and moral will but also of the created order itself.

Thus the systematic application of reason to a variety of intellectual undertakings, including economic problems, was not the invention of the Enlightenment. Rather, the application of reason within a coherent intellectual framework is the legacy of Christian scholasticism—the method of the medieval and early modern schools. The application of this scholastic method led to increased understanding of the world and human affairs, and spurred efforts to formulate logical explanations of regular occurrences in nature. "All things possess order amongst themselves: this order is the form that makes the world resemble God," wrote Dante in the *Divine Comedy*.[6] It can be argued that the specific application of scholastic method to economic problems became the seedbed for innovative ideas that, after much dialectical refinement, came to shape the world of modern economics. The truth of this statement does not rest on modernity's own understanding of its birth, development, or future

---

5. See Chris L. Firestone and Nathan Jacobs, eds., *The Persistence of the Sacred in Modern Thought* (Notre Dame: University of Notre Dame Press, 2011).

6. Dante, *Paradise*, trans. Anthony Esolen (New York: Modern Library, 2004), 1:103–5, p. 9.

trajectory but rather on the demonstrable "internal interconnections and affinities among ideas, their dynamism or 'particular go' (Lovejoy's phrase), and the logical pressures they are capable of exerting on the minds of those that think them."[7]

Assent to this claim, however, will require the positivist historian to reconsider not only the relationship between metaphysical schemata and intellectual traditions, which, in turn, will require an acknowledgement of the indispensable role of theological doctrines in the history of ideas,[8] but it will also require an admission that the recent detachment of economics from morality is itself a novelty, an aberration from a long-standing tradition within political economy itself.[9] In Alvey's judgment,

---

7. Francis Oakley, *Natural Law, Laws of Nature, Natural Rights: Continuity and Discontinuity in the History of Ideas* (New York and London: Continuum, 2005), 9.

8. See Oakley, *Natural Law, Laws of Nature, Natural Rights*, 13–34. See also the various essays in Oakley's *Politics and Eternity: Studies in the History of Medieval and Early-Modern Political Thought* (Leiden: Brill, 1999); Oakley, *Omnipotence, Covenant, and Order: An Excursion in the History of Ideas from Abelard to Leibniz* (Ithaca: Cornell University Press, 1984); Oakley, *Kingship: The Politics of Enchantment* (Oxford: Blackwell Publishing, 2006); and William J. Courtenay, *Covenant and Causality in Medieval Thought: Studies in Philosophy, Theology, and Economic Practice* (London: Variorum Reprints, 1984).

9. Broadly, on the historical constriction and positivism of contemporary economic thinking, see John D. Mueller, *Redeeming Economics: Rediscovering the Missing Element* (Wilmington, DE: ISI Books, 2010). See also Jeffrey T. Young, *Economics as a Moral Science: The Political Economy of Adam Smith* (Cheltenham, UK: Edward Elgar, 1997); James Alvey, "A Short History of Economics as a Moral Science," *Journal of Markets & Morality* 2, no. 1 (Spring 1999): 53–73; Ricardo F. Crespo, "Is Economics a Moral Science?," *Journal of Markets & Morality* 1, no. 2 (Fall 1998): 201–11; Peter J. Boettke, "Is Economics a Moral Science? A Response to Ricardo F. Crespo," *Journal of Markets & Morality* 1, no. 2 (Fall 1998): 212–19; and Crespo, "Is Economics a Moral Science? A Response to Peter J. Boettke," *Journal of Markets & Morality* 1, no. 2 (Fall 1998): 220–25; Jeffrey T. Young, *Econom-*

> There are two major reasons why economics has become
> detached from moral concerns. First, the natural sciences
> came to be seen as successful, and the attempt was made
> to emulate that success in economics by applying natural
> science methods, including mathematics, to economic phe-
> nomena. Second, the self-styled economic science came to
> adopt positivism, which ruled out moral issues from science
> itself.[10]

It is the latter recognition, perhaps more than any other, that
squares the revisionists off against the positivists in the debate
over the prehistory of economics.

When the positivistic bias begins to be put aside and we look
anew at works from earlier periods, we find the early modern
era to be a rich source of intellectual ferment on economic,
ethical, and legal and political topics. In the sixteenth and early
seventeenth centuries, a small but influential group of theologians
and jurists centered in Spain attempted to synthesize the Roman
legal texts with Aristotelian and Thomistic moral philosophy.
The movement began with the revival of Thomistic philosophy
in Paris, where, as Camacho recounts, "Pierre Crockaert under-
went an intellectual conversion from nominalist philosophy to
the philosophy of Thomas Aquinas."[11]

Shortly before 1225, the year of Aquinas' birth, Aristotle's works
on metaphysics, physics, politics, and ethics became available in
the West, and, within the span of a generation, Aristotelianism,
which had been brought to Europe by Arabic scholars, would
be a serious contender in medieval thought. Thomas sought

---

ics as a Moral Science: The Political Economy of Adam Smith (Cheltenham,
UK: Edward Elgar, 1997).

10. Alvey, "A Short History of Economics as a Moral Science," 53.

11. Francisco Gómez Camacho, "Later Scholastics: Spanish Economic
Thought in the Sixteenth and Seventeenth Centuries," in *Ancient and
Medieval Economic Ideas and Concepts of Social Justice*, ed. S. Todd Lowry
and Barry Gordon (Leiden and New York: Brill, 1998), 503.

a rapprochement between the Greek philosophical tradition that Aristotle represented and the Christian divine ideas tradition articulated by the likes of Augustine, pseudo-Dionysius, and Bonaventure. In 1512, Crockaert published his commentary on the last part of Thomas' *Summa theologica* with the help of a student, Francisco de Vitoria (ca. 1483–1546).[12]

Approximately two hundred years before Thomas was born, the *Corpus iuris civilis* of Justinian had been rediscovered and had become the object of academic disputation. However, the traditions of Roman law and Aristotelian and Thomistic philosophy existed in relative isolation from one other, at least until the early sixteenth century in Spain. "In the sixteenth and early seventeenth centuries," states Camacho, "a synthesis was finally achieved by that group of theologians and jurists known to historians of law as the 'late scholastics' or the 'Spanish natural law school.'"[13] Schumpeter concurs with this judgment and adds, "It is within their systems of moral theology and law that economics gained definite if not separate existence, and it is they who come nearer than does any other group to having been the 'founders' of scientific economics."[14] The Salamancans in particular, writes Moss,

---

12. Camacho, "Later Scholastics: Spanish Economic Thought in the Sixteenth and Seventeenth Centuries," 503.

13. Camacho, "Later Scholastics: Spanish Economic Thought in the Sixteenth and Seventeenth Centuries," 503.

14. Joseph Schumpeter, *History of Economic Analysis*, ed. Elizabeth Booty Schumpeter (Oxford: Oxford University Press, 1954), 97: "And not only that it will appear, even, that the bases they laid for a serviceable and well-integrated body of analytic tools and propositions were sounder than was much subsequent work, in the sense that a considerable part of the economics of the later nineteenth century might have been developed from those bases more quickly and with less trouble than it actually cost to develop it, and that some of that subsequent work was therefore in the nature of a time- and labor-consuming detour."

were as interested in a general theory of how exchange rates between different currencies are formed as in explaining why a bill of exchange is worth more in one region of Spain than in another region. Was the *agio* or exchange premium evidence of usury and therefore immoral behavior on the part of merchants and traders, or rather something 'natural' governed by the basic laws of supply and demand?[15]

The case of this so-called School of Salamanca is just one example of the rich intellectual traditions that have far too often been ignored or downplayed by contemporary scholarship. The coherent intellectual framework of Christian scholasticism reverberates not only in the field of economics but also in the related areas of ethics and law. Thus, political theorists John Neville Figgis and Otto von Gierke drew on the work of a variety of sixteenth- and seventeenth-century Dutch, Swiss, German, and Spanish jurists and ethicists who articulated concepts that laid the foundation for federalist political structures, constitutionalism, popular sovereignty, natural-law jurisprudence, and limited government in the Western legal tradition.[16] The diversity and variety of relevant sources from this period is underscored by the contribution of Protestant scholars, who produced significant scholastic works as well as more occasional treatises. Much of the early Protestant thought on economics, ethics, and law attaches to their homiletical and exegetical work in addition to the achievements in systems of moral theology and philosophy. The Dutch Reformed legal thinker Johannes Althusius (1563–1638) stands as a representative example in this regard, and his contributions

---

15. Laurence S. Moss, "Introduction," in *Economic Thought in Spain: Selected Essays of Marjorie Grice-Hutchinson*, ed. Laurence S. Moss and Christopher K. Ryan (Brookfield, VT: Edward Elgar, 1993), xv.

16. On Johannes Althusius in particular, see Otto von Gierke, *The Development of Political Theory*, trans. Bernard Freyd (New York: Howard Fertig, 1966), 70; and John Neville Figgis, *Studies of Political Thought: From Gerson to Grotius, 1414–1625* (Cambridge: Cambridge University Press, 1907), 175–85.

to the development of Western legal and political traditions are becoming increasingly appreciated.[17] After a long period in which economics, ethics, and law became detached from theology, many economists, legal scholars, political theorists, and theologians now see the benefit of studying early modern economic, ethical, and legal texts in their full cultural, often religious, context.

The Sources in Early Modern Economics, Ethics, and Law series is the latest installment in the excavation of the mines of early modern theological thought on these topics. The aim of this series is to offer economists, intellectual historians, moral theologians, and graduate students in the fields of economics, economic ethics, economic history, banking history, political economy, and moral theology a useful and accessible collection of some of the most important early modern texts in the fields of economics, ethics, and law. Now, for the first time, the unabridged texts of works such as Martín de Azpilcueta's *Commentary on the Resolution of Money* (1556), Luis de Molina's *Treatise on Money* (1597), and Juan de Mariana's *Treatise on the Alteration of Money* (1609), as well as selections from larger works such as Johannes Althusius' *Dicaeologicae* (1617) and Girolamo Zanchi's *Omnium operum theologicorum* (1619) will be available as stand-alone volumes in English translation and in modern editions with scholarly annotations. We hope that the publication of these primary texts in a series of paperbacks will help to facilitate exploration of the continuities and discontinuities, agreements and disagreements, innovations and ruptures among

---

17. See, for instance, John Witte Jr., "A Demonstrative Theory of Natural Law: The Original Contribution of Johannes Althusius," in *Public Theology for a Global Society: Essays in Honor of Max L. Stackhouse*, ed. Deirdre King Hainsworth and Scott R. Paeth (Grand Rapids: Eerdmans, 2010), 21–36; and Thomas O. Hueglin, *Early Modern Concepts for a Late Medieval World: Althusius on Community and Federalism* (Waterloo, ON: Wilfrid Laurier University Press, 1999).

theological communities during the latter half of the sixteenth and the early seventeenth century.

The translations and modern editions (in conjunction with the introductions by leading authorities) will show the sophistication with which Christian thinkers from a variety of confessional and theological perspectives examined issues such as the role and responsibilities of the civil magistrates, the existence and efficacy of natural law, usury, and the ethics of moneylending, as well as the new process of using bills of exchange (*cambium per litteras*) to replace the cumbersome and dangerous transportation of metallic coins between commercial fairs, which led not only to new scholastic insights on interest, credit, and international trade but also to a much more comprehensive analysis of monetary exchange and banking practices than had been undertaken before. The texts will also address the questions as particular as why the same currency was worth more in one region than another area's currency, and, moreover, why the rate of exchange fluctuated between one area and the next. These moral and economic concerns, along with many others, will be addressed in detail throughout the course of the series by some of the leading, and heretofore underappreciated, authorities from the early modern era.

ABBREVIATIONS

BNP—*Brill's New Pauly: Encyclopaedia of the Ancient World*, 22 vols. (Leiden: Brill, 2002–2011)

BU—*Biographie Universelle, ancienne et moderne; ou Histoire, par ordre alphabétique, de la vie publique et privée de tous les hommes qui se sont fait remarquer par leurs écrits, leurs actions, leurs talents, leurs vertus our leurs crimes*, ed. J. Fr. Michaud and L. G. Michaud, 85 vols. (Paris: Michaud freres [etc.], 1811–1862)

CE—*The Catholic Encyclopedia: An International Work of Reference on the Constitution, Doctrine, Discipline, and History of the Catholic Church*, ed. Charles G. Herbermann et al., 17 vols. (New York: The Encyclopedia Press, 1840–1916)

DMA—*Dictionary of the Middle Ages*, ed. Joseph R. Strayer, 13 vols. (New York: Scribner, 1982–1986)

DNP—*Der Neue Pauly: Enzyklopadie der Antike*, ed. Hubert Cancik, Helmut Schneider, and Manfred Landfester, 16 vols. (Stuttgart: J. B. Metzler, 1996–2003)

EB—*The Encyclopaedia Brittannica: A Dictionary of Arts, Sciences, Literature, and General Information*, ed. Hugh Chisholm, 11th ed., 32 vols. (New York: The Encyclopaedia Brittannica Company, 1910–1911)

ERE—*Encyclopedia of Religion and Ethics*, ed. James Hastings, 13 vols. (New York: Charles Scribner's Sons; Edinburgh, T. & T. Clark, 1911–1922)

EtR—*Encyclopedia of the Renaissance*, ed. Paul F. Grendler, 6 vols. (New York: Scribner's published in association with the Renaissance Society of America, 1999)

Nbg—*Nouvelle biographie générale depuis les temps les plus reculés jusqu'à nos jours, avec les renseignements bibliographiques et l'indication des sources a consulter; publiee par mm. Firmin Didot freres, sous la direction de m. le dr. Hoefer*, ed. M. Jean Chrétien Ferdinand Hoefer, 46 vols. (Copenhagen: Rosenkilde et Bagger, 1963, repr. of the 1857 ed.)

NCE—*New Catholic Encyclopedia*, prepared by an editorial staff at the Catholic University of America, 18 vols. (New York: McGraw-Hill, 1967–1988)

NCIRE—*The New Century Italian Renaissance Encyclopedia*, ed. Catherine B. Avery (New York: Appleton-Century-Crofts, 1972)

OCD—*The Oxford Classical Dictionary*, ed. Simon Hornblower and Antony Spawforth, 3rd edition (New York: Oxford University Press, 1996)

INTRODUCTION

Alejandro A. Chafuen

Lord Acton stated that "the greater part of the political ideas of Milton, Locke, and Rousseau may be found in the ponderous Latin of Jesuits."[1] The Late Scholastic period (approximately 1300–1600 AD) generated some of the most detailed moral analyses of social issues ever produced by Christian writers. In particular, the moral theologians working from, and around, the University of Salamanca in Spain offered penetrating insights into economics, politics, and other social concerns. Prominent among the Latin Jesuits was Father Juan de Mariana.

Juan de Mariana, SJ (1536–1624) was one of the most extraordinary persons of his time.[2] He achieved acclaim for his works *On Monarchy* (*De rege et regis institutione*)[3] and *History*

1. John Dalberg Acton, *The History of Freedom and Other Essays* (New York: Classics of Liberty Library, 1993 [1907]), 82.

2. For an excellent biography, see G. Kasten Tallmadge, "Juan de Mariana," in *Jesuit Thinkers of the Renaissance*, ed. Gerard Smith (Milwaukee: Marquette University Press, 1939), 157–92.

3. Juan de Mariana, *The King and the Education of the King*, trans. G. A. Moore (Chevy Chase, MD: Country Dollar Press, 1948). Moore's introduction is a superb analysis of Mariana's life.

of Spain.[4] John Neville Figgis wrote concerning one chapter of Mariana's book on the monarchy: "The course of the argument is singularly instructive, and much of it might have been written by Locke."[5] Mariana's treatise on money presented here also should have earned him a reputation as one of the most profound economic thinkers of his period.

While pursuing my economic education, I had the privilege of studying and living in the area where Mariana spent most of his life—Toledo, in the heart of Castile. Walking the same cobblestone streets, trekking across the countryside where luxurious villas still dot the landscape as they did in Mariana's day, one cannot but notice the confluence of Jewish, Muslim, and Christian cultures. When one reads Mariana's *History of Spain*, one enters the heart of this rich cultural mix. Reading *On Monarchy*, one gets inside the palaces, court disputes, and the dilemmas of authority that characterized the day.

When Mariana was twenty-three years old, just before his ordination, he was asked to teach philosophy and theology at the prestigious Roman College. It was there that he had Saint Robert Cardinal Bellarmine, SJ, as a student.[6] Bellarmine spent eleven years teaching at the Roman College (starting in 1576). Bellarmine, who was later made a cardinal and canonized, had political beliefs similar to those of Mariana. Their ideas have been regarded by many as having influenced some of the

---

4. Juan de Mariana, *History of Spain*, trans. Captain John Stevens (London: Richard Sare, Francis Saunders, and Thomas Bennett, 1699).

5. Figgis wrote further: "It is notable that, although deciding in chapter 2 that monarchy is the best form of government, Mariana would yet surround his king with all sorts of limitations, so that he really leaves the sovereignty with the people." See John Neville Figgis, *The Divine Right of Kings*, 2nd ed. (Cambridge: Cambridge University Press, 1922), 219–20.

6. Lord Acton described Bellarmine as "the most famous controversialist of the sixteenth century" and "one of the masters of revolutionary Catholicism, and a forerunner of Algernon Sidney." See Acton, *Lectures on Modern History* (London: Macmillan, 1929), 169.

intellectual movements behind the founding of the American Republic. More generally, the Jesuits were seen as influencing the turn in the seventeenth and eighteenth centuries away from the theory and practice of despotism by divine right and toward the rehabilitation of medieval notions of natural rights and duties, constitutionalism, and popular sovereignty.[7]

When he was thirty-three, Mariana was asked to teach at the University of Paris, the most renowned institution of higher learning at the time. Health problems, however, forced him to return to Spain only four years later. It was there that he wrote his *History of Spain* and his treatise *On Monarchy* (1599). The work, requested by Philip II and dedicated to Philip III, gained notoriety upon the assassination of Henry IV of France in 1610. Mariana's argument that kingly power derives from the people, some believed, had provided justification for tyrannicide. In some circles Mariana became an unpopular figure, especially in France. Unsurprisingly, Henry IV's assassin had never heard of him. J. Balmés questions: "Is it not, therefore, remarkable, that the famous book [*De rege*] … which was burned at Paris by the hand of the public executioner, had been published in Spain eleven years before, without the least obstacle to its publication, either on the part of the ecclesiastical or civil authority?"[8]

Mariana further immersed himself in controversy with the publication of his attack on monetary debasement and accusation of fraud against Spanish fiscal officials.[9] The last decade of his life was more peaceful, as he confined himself to a scholarly treatment of Scripture. Mariana died in Toledo in 1624. Talavera, his place of birth, honored him with a monument in 1888.

---

7. See, for instance, Moorhouse F. X. Millar, "Scholasticism and American Political Philosophy," in *Present-Day Thinkers and the New Scholasticism*, ed. John S. Zybura (St. Louis: Herder, 1927), 301–41.

8. J. Balmés, *European Civilization: Protestantism and Catholicity* [*sic*] *Compared*, 3rd ed. (London: Burns and Lambert, 1861), 296.

9. *New Catholic Encyclopedia*, s.v. "Mariana, Juan de."

Our present volume, Mariana's treatise on currency debasement, gives the reader a glimpse of Mariana's knowledge of history and political science, tackling the topic with an economic profundity that I have not been able to find in any other previous work on political economy.

Given contemporary specialization in the academy, many readers might at first be puzzled as to why a moral theologian would write a treatise on money. The Scholastic thinkers were, however, men of wide and deep knowledge. For most of them, moral analysis was their primary concern. Yet, as good moral theologians, they understood that performing proper moral analysis requires a practical understanding of the matter at hand. If one wants to understand just prices and fairness in market exchanges, one first has to understand price theory and how a market operates. In Mariana's case, the issue before him was monetary policy and its effects on the common good of the kingdom.[10] He wrote this treatise to offer his insights to the king, advising him on how to protect the economic well-being of the land. As such, it is not only a moral examination of monetary policy but also a brilliant economic treatise.

Mariana is still best known for his historical contributions. John Laures, SJ, wrote that Mariana's *History of Spain* "is still considered a masterpiece of classical Spanish style."[11] Nor did his historical work pass unnoticed by the Founding Fathers of America. In fact, Thomas Jefferson recommended and sent Mariana's *History of Spain* to James Madison.[12] Yet, Edwin R. A.

---

10. The treatise on the alteration of money (*De monetae mutatione*) was published in a collection of seven treatises by Mariana, *Tractatus VII* (Cologne: Antonij Hierati, 1609).

11. John Laures, *The Political Economy of Juan de Mariana* (New York: Fordham University Press, 1928), 3.

12. *Jefferson: Autobiography, Notes on the State of Virginia, Public and Private Papers, Addresses, Letters* (New York: Library of America, 1984), 820–25.

Seligman states in the introduction to Laures's study on Mariana's monetary theories: "Mariana's fame or, rather, his notoriety as a defender of monarchy, has caused the modern world entirely to overlook his substantial achievement in the field of economics."[13]

Still, Mariana's attributes as an economist were rightly noted by Oscar Jàszi and John D. Lewis, who, in their work of political science, *Against the Tyrant*, stated that Mariana was an "acute political economist."[14] Mariana's major topic as an economist—monetary theory—was a controversial one in the context of sixteenth- and seventeenth-century monarchical absolutism. George Albert Moore, in his outstanding introduction to Mariana's *De rege et regis institutione*, explains the hazards of the subject matter:

> The *De monetae mutatione* likewise was a dangerous subject, for, as Bodin points out in his Response to Malestroit's *Paradoxes*, this matter of depreciating the currency was the peculiar graft of the kings and princes. This tract caused him to be imprisoned from four months to a year, the loss of his papers, which it seems were never returned to him, a threat of dire action by the dread Inquisition, and all this in his advanced age.[15]

Henry Hallam, the great historian of the Middle Ages, labeled the usual practice of monetary debasement as an "extensive plan of rapine" and "as mingled fraud and robbery."[16] Castelot, writing about Mariana in the *Palgrave's Dictionary of Political Economy*, also mentions that this writing caused him to be "confined for a year in the convent in Madrid." In spite of opposition, in *De monetae* Mariana "fearlessly maintained that 'the king, having

---

13. Laures, *Political Economy*, v.

14. Oscar Jàszi and John D. Lewis, *Against the Tyrant* (Glencoe, IL: Free Press, 1957), 68.

15. *The King and the Education of the King*, 79–80.

16. Henry Hallam, *View of the State of Europe during the Middle Ages*, 4th ed. (London: Alex Murray and Son, 1868), 110–11.

no right to tax his subjects without their consent,' had no right to lower the weight or quality of the coinage without their acquiescence."[17] In an era in which monarchs regularly abused monetary power at the expense of their nation's citizens, Mariana defended those citizens and demanded responsible use of the government mints.

In this treatise, we find an insightful analysis concerning how monetary debasement and inflation increase prices, which proceeds to illustrate how such increases do not affect everyone equally—in effect, causing a revolution in fortunes. In a parallel argument, Mariana explains how government, if given control of other forms of private property, would also debase the values of those forms and use them according to its own interests.

Mariana understood that currency debasement threatened the entire economic order of the kingdom. Property rights, the ability to trade goods and services, and fair wages—all of these things require stable currency. To cite Mariana:

> [Thus,] if a prince is not empowered to levy taxes on unwilling subjects, and cannot set up monopolies for merchandise, he is not empowered to make fresh profit from debased money. These strategies aim at the same thing: cleaning out the pockets of the people and piling up money in the provincial treasury. Do not be taken in by the smoke and mirrors by which metal is given a greater value than it has by nature and in common estimation. Of course, this does not happen without common injury. When blood is let by whatever device or strategy, the body will certainly be debilitated and wasted. In the same way, a prince cannot profit without the suffering and groans of his subjects.[18]

---

17. Castelot, "Juan de Mariana, SJ," in *Palgrave's Dictionary of Political Economy* (London: Macmillan, 1926), 2:692.

18. Juan de Mariana, *A Treatise on the Alteration of Money*, trans. Patrick T. Brannan (Grand Rapids: CLP Academic, 2011), 24.

A short-sighted optimism caused by a reduction in monetary debasement during the last decade of the twentieth century might lessen the impact of this English edition of Mariana's treatise on currency debasement. Yet, governments throughout the world still regard the control of money as an essential tool and sometimes use it to debauch their citizens rather than to protect them. Reading this text, one is struck by the urgency of Mariana's entreaties as he bluntly challenges his reader to show him where his analysis is wrong.

Why, one may ask, does Mariana's text have such an urgency, so much so that he is prepared to use awkward phrasing or avoid detailed explanation of certain events and matters because Mariana is, as he himself states, "hurrying to end this discussion"? For one thing, the perils emanating from currency debasement that Spain and its empire faced at the time of this treatise's composition were great. Calamities had befallen the kingdoms of the Iberian peninsula in the past as a result of debasement. Hence, we discover Mariana stating, "What has happened will happen. Previous events are very influential: They convince us that what sets out on the same path will reach the same conclusion."[19]

However, also blended into this treatise are constant references to the manner in which the act of currency debasement defies "right reason." This is not coincidental. Like others from the School of Salamanca, Mariana belonged to the natural-law tradition, of which the Roman Catholic Church has been the staunchest defender for almost two thousand years. In short, the evil of currency debasement is derived from deeper sources than its consequences. To Mariana's mind, the very act of currency debasement is *in itself* evil; this would be true even if such acts had no apparent ill effects (such as increasing the cost of trade). In Mariana's treatise, we do not find a trace of the consequentialist mentality that has proved so destructive of sound moral

---

19. Mariana, *A Treatise on the Alteration of Money*, 59.

thinking since the nineteenth century.[20] The act of defrauding people is, in each and every instance, *wrong* and consequently threatens the salvation of persons engaging in such activity. This sobering thought is perhaps Mariana's most important warning to those contemplating such action today.

20. For a devastating critique of consequentialism, see John Finnis, *Natural Law and Natural Rights* (Oxford: Oxford University Press, 1993), 112–19, 131–32.

A TREATISE ON THE
ALTERATION OF MONEY

ARGUMENT

At the time that there was a great shortage of money in Spain and the treasury was completely exhausted by long and drawn-out wars in many places and by many other problems, many ways to make up for this shortage were thought out and tried. Among others, consideration was given to the debasing of money, and that in two ways. First, by doubling the value of existing money, the king gained a good deal: half of the entire sum, which was huge—a great profit in the situation! Second, new money was minted from pure copper with no addition of silver, as was customary. Rather, their weight was diminished by half. In this way, the king profited by more than two-thirds. Men's plans are not provident. Seduced by present abundance, they gave no consideration to the plan's inherent evils into which they were rushing. There were, however, those who were more cautious because of their knowledge of history and past evils, and they criticized this approach within their own circles and even in writing. Very soon, events proved that they were not foolish prophets. Things got worse. Some convenient reason was being sought for destroying or recalling that money. Some consultants recommended the debasement of silver money to make up, with that profit, for the loss that they saw was necessarily coming because of the old copper money. The cure was more deadly than the disease. It has been rejected until the present. Rather, there was a recent decree recalling a large part of the new money and for compensating the owners from the royal revenues. Such was the occasion for a new effort to publish this treatise, which we began earlier. It aims at letting other generations learn from our misfortunes that money is hardly ever debased without calamity to the state: Profit for the moment is intimately connected with manifold ruin along with rather great disadvantages.[1]

---

1. In this case of Mariana's *Treatise on the Alteration of Money*, Fr. Brannan translated from the Latin text of *De monetae mutatione* (1609), which John Laures, SJ, faithfully reproduced and published in an appendix to *The Political Economy of Juan de Mariana* (New York: Fordham University Press, 1928), 241–303. Fr. Laures based his reproduction on the first and only available edition of *De monetae mutatione* found in *Tractatus VII* (Cologne: Antonij Hierati, 1609), 189–221. Extensive refinements and additions to Fr. Brannan's translation have been made in this edition, including the addition of these editorial notes as well as in paragraphing and the spelling of names, places, and book titles, which have been changed to conform with Josef Falzberger's recently published critical edition of *De monetae* in Latin and German: Ioannes Mariana, *De monetae mutatione (MDCIX)* = Juan de Mariana, *Über die Münzveränderung (1609)*, ed. Josef Falzberger (Heidelberg: Manutius, 1996).

PREFACE

May the immortal God and all his saints grant that my labors may benefit the public, as I have always prayed. The only reward that I seek and wish is that our king, his advisers, and other royal ministers entrusted with the administration of affairs may carefully read this pamphlet. Here I have clearly, if not elegantly, attempted to illustrate certain excesses and abuses, which, I think, must be strenuously avoided. The point at issue is that copper money, as minted in the province today, is of inferior quality to earlier coins.

Indeed, this practice inspired me to begin and complete this slight, but not insignificant, endeavor without consideration of men's judgment. Doubtless, some will indict me for boldness and others for rash confidence. However, reckless of danger, I do not hesitate to condemn and revile things that men of greater prudence and experience considered a cure for ills. Nonetheless, my sincere desire to help will deliver me in part from such accusations and faults, and the fact of the matter is that nothing expressed in this controversy is original with me. When the entire nation, old and young, rich and poor, educated and uneducated is shouting and groaning under this burden, it should not seem remarkable that from this multitude someone dares to put in writing something that is censured with some emotion in public and in secret gatherings; in squares and the streets. If nothing else, I shall fulfill the rightful duty that a well-read man should exercise in the state because he is not unaware of what has happened in the history of the world.[1]

---

1. The economist Murray Rothbard recounts the fascinating saga surrounding Mariana's *De monetae mutatione*, which is reproduced here (See Murray N. Rothbard, *Economic Thought Before Adam Smith: An Austrian Perspective on the History of Economic Thought*, vol. 1 [Brookfield, VT: Edward Elgar Publishing Company, 1995], 121). Mariana's tract, which attacks King Philip II's debasement of the currency, led the monarch to haul the aged (seventy-three-year-old) scholar-priest into prison, charging him with the high crime of treason against the king. He was convicted of the crime, but the pope refused to punish him. He was released from prison after four months on the condition that he would remove the offensive passages in the work, and would promise to be more careful in the future.

King Philip, however, was not satisfied with the pope's punishment. So the king ordered his officials to buy up every copy they could find and to destroy them. After Mariana's death, the Spanish Inquisition expurgated the remaining copies, deleting many sentences and smearing entire pages with ink. All non-expurgated copies were put on the Spanish *Index*, and these in turn were expurgated during the course of the seventeenth century. As a result of Philip's censorship, the existence of the Latin text remained unknown for 250 years, and was rediscovered only because the Spanish edition, which Mariana himself had translated into Spanish, was incorporated into a nineteenth-century collection of classical Spanish essays: Juan de Mariana, *Tratado y discurso sobre la moneda de vellón*, estudio introductorio, Lucas Beltrán (Madrid: Ministerio de Economía y Hacienda/ Instituto de Estudios Fiscales, 1987). Mariana's original Spanish title was *Tratado y discurso sobre la moneda de vellón que al presente se labra en Castilla y de algunos desórdenes y abusos*. Hence, few complete copies of the original survive. One can be found digitally courtesy of the Austrian National Library, while another can be found in the United States at the Boston Public Library.

The famous city of Corinth, as Lucian[2] tells us, knew from reports and rumors that Philip of Macedon[3] was hastening against it in arms. The citizens, in fear, acted swiftly: Some prepared arms, others fortified the walls, and others prepared provisions and instruments of war. Diogenes the Cynic[4] was living in that city, and when he saw that he was not invited to have any part in the work and preparation and was considered useless by everyone, he came out of the barrel in which he used to live and began to roll it quite eagerly up and down. The citizens, indignant inasmuch as he seemed to make fun of the common

2. Lucian of Samosata (ca. 120–180 AD), was a Greek satirist who traveled widely as a rhetorician until approximately 165, when he left rhetoric to study philosophy and write in Athens. He composed eighty prose pieces in various forms—essays, speeches, letters, dialogues, and stories—in which he satirically portrayed the manners, morals, and beliefs of Athenians. His writing was influenced by Aristophanes, Theophrastus, and Menippus. His amusing burlesques of myths, poets, and historians; of bluff, cheating, and necromancy, made him a favorite of Renaissance humanists (NCE, 8, 1058, s.v. Lucian of Samosata). A fuller account of Corinth's attack can be found in Thucydides' *Peloponnesian War* (II.91–95), on which Lucian's report is likely based.

3. Philip II of Macedon (382–336 BC), father of Alexander the Great and conqueror of Greece, Illyria, and Thrace, ruled Macedonia from 359–336. After the Battle of Chariots described in Thucydides' *Peloponnesian War* Corinth became a Macedonian garrison.

4. Diogenes the Cynic (ca. 400–325 BC), after his arrival in Athens, seems to have been attracted by the austere character and way of life of Antisthenes, which perhaps influenced him in his fanatical espousal of the "natural" life, the subject of many anecdotes. While in Athens he was reputed to have lived in a tub (of earthenware) belonging to Metroon (temple of the Mother of the gods). Later, while on a voyage, he was captured by pirates and sold as a slave to a Corinthian. This is how he ended up in Corinth, which is where he is said to have met Alexander the Great. For him, happiness consists in satisfying only the most elementary needs of food and shelter, living on one's own natural endowments, and renouncing all possessions and relationships. Physical and mental self-discipline is the key to achieving the kind of self-sufficiency Diogenes sought. (OCD, 473–74, s.v. Diogenes the Cynic)

calamity, asked him what he was doing. He answered, "It is not right for me alone to be at leisure when everyone else is busy." At Athens again, as Plutarch[5] tells us, when there was civil unrest and all parties were bent on revolution, Solon,[6] no longer able to help the fatherland because of his age, took his stand in arms before the doors of his house, to show that he wished to help despite his lack of physical strength. Ezekiel[7] says that even the trumpeter does his duty if, at the appointed times, he blows into his instrument and his blast sounds—now attack, now retreat—at

---

5. Plutarch (ca. 46–ca. 120 AD), Greek biographer, historian, and moral philosopher, studied philosophy at Athens under the Platonist Ammonius. He is the author of a series of fifty biographies known as *Parallel Lives* in which he relates the life of some eminent Greek (statesmen or soldier) followed by the life of some similar Roman offering some points of resemblance, and then a short comparison of the two. He includes biographies of such people as Solon, Themistocles, Aristeides, Pericles, Alcibiades, Demosthenes, Alexander, Pyrrhus, Pompey, Mark Antony, Brutus, Julius Caesar, Cicero, and others. Plutarch's object in the *Lives* is to bring out a subject's moral character, rather than to recount the political events of the time. However, besides interesting anecdotes, the *Lives* contain memorable historical passages related to specific events in the Peloponnesian War such as the one Mariana recounts of Solon. (OCD, 1200–1201, s.v. Plutarch)

6. Solon (ca. 640–after 561 BC), Athenian statesman and poet, wrote elegiac and iambic poetry to publicize and justify his political policies. He was elected archon in 594/593 at a time when Athens was on the brink of revolution, largely because of an agrarian system in which landowners grew rich and the poor were reduced to slavery. Solon's moderate and humane reforms helped to produce the constitutional framework that made the eventual transition to democratic rule easier. In a famous reply to the poet Mimnermus, who had said that he wanted to die when he reached sixty, Solon declared that the poet should rather say eighty. This remark should probably be taken in conjunction with another famous line by Solon to the effect that even as he grows old he still continues to learn. (OCD, 1421–22, s.v. Solon)

7. Ezekiel was an Old Testament prophet who was among the Jews exiled to Babylon by King Nebuchadnezzar in 597 BC. Ezekiel was a man of broad knowledge not only of his own nation's history but also of international affairs and history. Mariana's reference is likely to Ezekiel 33:1–7.

the leader's command, even though the soldiers may not follow the commands.

At a time when some are restrained by fear, others held, as it were, in bondage by ambition, and a few are losing their tongues and stopping their mouths because of gold and gifts, this pamphlet will achieve at least one goal: All will understand that there is someone among the people who defends the truth in his retirement and points out the public threat of dangers and evils if they are not confronted with dispatch. Finally, like Diogenes, I will appear in public, I will rattle my barrel; I will openly assert what I think—whatever the final outcome. Perhaps my earnest activity will be of some use, since everyone desires the truth and is eager to help. May my readers be open to this instruction. It was undertaken with a sincere heart. To this end, I pray to our Heavenly Majesty and to our earthly majesty who is his vicar and to all the citizens of heaven as well. Furthermore, I earnestly entreat men of every condition and dignity not to condemn my undertaking, or pass negative judgment on it, before they have read this pamphlet carefully and assiduously examined the question at issue. In my opinion, it is the most serious of issues to arise in Spain in many years.

1

DOES THE KING OWN HIS SUBJECTS' GOODS?

Many enhance kingly power beyond reasonable and just limits—some to gain the prince's favor and some to amass private wealth. These most pestilent of men are not concerned with honesty and are commonly found in the courts of princes. Others reason to the conviction that an increase in royal majesty enhances the protection of public welfare. However, they are mistaken. As in the case of other virtues, power has definite limits, and when it goes beyond limits, power does not become stronger but rather becomes completely debilitated and breaks down. As the experts say, power is not like money. The more gold that one amasses, the richer and happier one is. Power, rather, is like nourishment; the stomach groans equally if it lacks food or is burdened with too much food. It is bothered in either case.

Royal power increased beyond its limits is proven to degenerate into tyranny, a form of government that is not only base but also weak and short-lived. No power and no arms can withstand the fury of its offended subjects and enemies. Surely, the very nature of royal power—if it is legitimate and just, arising from the state—makes clear that the king is not the owner of his subjects' private possessions. He has not been given the power to fall upon their houses and lands and to seize and set aside what he will. According to Aristotle, the first thing that brought kings to eminence was their protection of citizens from the impending enemy storms when their people were mustered around their standards.[1] Thereafter, in time of peace, they were given in time the power to punish the guilty and the authority to settle all litigation among their people. To protect this authority in a dignified manner, the people established fixed revenue by which the kings could support their original lifestyle, and they decided how this money was to be paid. This process establishes the king's right of ownership over those revenues that the state conferred, as well as of those possessions that he acquired as a private citizen or that he received from the people after becoming king. However, he does not exercise dominion over those things that the citizens have kept either publicly or privately to themselves, for neither the power conferred upon the leader in time of war nor the authority to govern subjects grants the authorization to take possession of the goods of individuals. Thus, in the chapter of the *Novellas constitutiones*, beginning "Regalia," which treats of all aspects of the royal office, such dominion is not found.[2]

---

1. Aristotle (384–322 BC) was a student of Plato and later founded his own peripatetic school of philosophy. Moreover, he was also Alexander the Great's private tutor. Aristotle developed a comprehensive philosophy that encompassed such domains as logic, physics (natural science and metaphysics), ethics, and politics. Mariana is likely referring to bk. 5, chap. 10, nos. 1–10 in Aristotle's *Politics*.

2. *Novellae* are authoritative determinations (such as laws, edicts, and judgments) that actually provide legal supplements and have been compiled into the form of a digest. The exact date of composition of these short treatises and the binding force associated with the legal compilations was the so-called *Nueva Recopilación* (i.e., *Recopilación de leyes de estos Reynos*) of 1569. Prior to 1569, the Catholic rulers Ferdinand and Isabella assigned the title *Ordinamentum* to the collected *novellae*. (DMA, 7, 429–30, s.v. Law Codes: 1000–1500; and DMA, 7, 522–23, s.v. Law, Spanish)

Indeed, if the possessions of all subjects were under the king's will, the actions of Jezebel, as she appropriated Naboth's vineyard, would not have been censured so severely.[3] If she had been just pursuing her own rights, or those of her husband who was certainly king, she would have been claiming what was her own. Had this been true, Naboth would have been accused of contumacy for unjustly refusing to pay his debt. Therefore, it is the common opinion of legal experts (as they explain in the last law of the chapter, "Si contra ius vel utilitatem publicam"[4] and, as Panormitanus[5] presents it, in chapter 4, *De iureiurando*) that kings cannot ratify any law that would harm their subjects without the consent of their people. Specifically, it is criminal for kings to strip their people of their goods, or part of their goods, and to claim these goods as their own. Indeed, it would not be

---

3. The story of Naboth's vineyard can be found in 1 Kings 21.

4. Over time, numerous commentaries and handbooks (with varying degrees of authority) were written and appended to the *Nueva Recopilación*. In his Spanish translation of the work in question, Mariana assigned the title *De iuresdictione*.

5. Nicolò de' Tudeschi (1386–1445), also known as "abbas modernus" or "recentior," "abbas Panormitanus" or "Siculus," was a Benedictine canonist. In 1400, he entered the Order of Saint Benedict; he was sent to the University of Bologna to study under Zabarella. In 1411, he became a doctor of canon law and taught successively at Parma (1412–1418), Siena (1419–1430), and Bologna (1431–1432). Meanwhile in 1425, he was made abbot of the monastery of Maniacio, near Massina, whence his title "abbas." In 1434, he placed himself at the service of Alfonso of Castile, King of Sicily, obtaining the See of Palermo in 1435, whence his name "Panormitanus." During the troubles that plagued the pontificate of Eugene IV, Nicolò at first followed the party of the pontiff but subsequently allied himself with the papal contender Felix V who, in 1440, named him cardinal. In his *Tractatus de concilio Basileensi* he upheld the doctrine of the superiority of a general council to the pope. It was his canonical works, especially his commentary on the decretals of Pope Gregory IX that won him the title of *lucerna juris* ("lamp of the law") and insured him great authority; he also wrote *Consilia*, *Quaestiones*, *Repetitiones*, *Disputationes*, *disceptationes et allegationes*, and *Flores utriusque juris*. (CE, 11, 69, s.v. Nicolò de' Tudeschi)

legal to initiate a suit against the prince and to set a day for trial if everything were under his power and law. The response would be automatic: If he has stripped anyone of anything, he did not do it unjustly but of his own right. He would not purchase private homes or land when he needed them but would seize them as his own. It is useless to develop this obvious point further: Lies cannot destroy it; no flattery can present darkness as full day. On the one hand, it is the essence of a tyrant to set no limits to his power, to consider that he is master of all. A king, on the other hand, puts a limit to his authority, reins in his desires, makes decisions justly and equitably, and does not transgress. A king maintains that the goods of others are entrusted to him and under his protection and that he does not strip his people of their possessions except, perhaps, according to the prescripts and formalities of law.

2

CAN THE KING DEMAND TRIBUTE FROM HIS SUBJECTS WITHOUT THEIR CONSENT?

Some people deem it a serious matter and not in keeping with majesty to make the prince's treasury depend upon the will of the people so that he cannot demand new tribute from them without their consent. That is to say, it is a serious matter when the people, and not the king, become the judge and moderator of affairs. They go on to maintain that if the king summons a parliament in the kingdom when new taxes are imposed, this fact should be attributed to his modesty. He is able to levy taxes of his own volition, without even consulting his subjects, as affairs and fiscal necessity might demand. These pleasant words are dear to kingly ears, and they have sometimes led neighboring kings into error—witness the French kings.

In his biography of Louis XI, Philippus Comineus,[1] who lived during the aforementioned king's lifetime, writes that Louis XI's

---

1. Philippe de Comines (1447–1511) wrote the biography of Louis XI, King of France, which was originally titled: *Les mémoires de Messire Philippe de Commines, Chevalier, Seigneur d' Argenton sur les principaux faicts et gestes de Louis onzième et de Charles huictième, son fils, Roys de France*. Louis XI (1423–1483), the son of Charles VII and Mary of Anjou,

father was the first to follow this approach. Louis XI's father was none other than Charles VII.[2] Financial problems were especially pressing in the large part of the country occupied by the English. Charles VII placated the nobles with annual pensions, but he chose to oppress the rest of the people with new taxes. Since then, as the saying goes, the French kings came into their own but stopped protecting their people. After many years, the veritable wound that they received by offending the people has not healed; it is bloody even to this day. I might add that the recent French civil wars, waged so violently for so many years, arose from no other source.[3] For this, oppressed people—most

---

took the throne in 1461. Louis, due to a quarrel with his father in 1447, was living in exile in Burgundy when he succeeded to the throne in July 1461. Afterward, Louis set out to persecute his father's principal ministers, but Louis' Burgundian friends began to take advantage of his weaknesses. He then attempted to thwart the Burgundians through several costly efforts. After buying off Edward IV's invasion of France in 1475, he subsizied Swiss attacks on his father's loyal associates. To augment his revenue he encouraged French trade and industry and suppressed several independent fiefs when the direct lines died out. He abolished the Pragmatic Sanction but retained control of the Church as his father had. Louis was disliked for several reasons, not the least of which concerned his financial exactions, tyrannical manner, and diplomatic duplicity. (NCE, 8, 1012, s.v. Louis XI, King of France)

2. Charles VII (1403–1461) succeeded to the throne in 1422 as the fifth of the Valois dynasty. Charles VII, son of the insane Charles VI, inherited a divided France whose northern half was ruled by an Anglo-Burgundian coalition. Charles was largely unsuccessful in his attempt to overthrow the northern coalition until Joan of Arc appeared and raised the siege of Orléans. After Joan's capture (May 13, 1430) inactivity followed, but in 1435 Philip the Fair, Duke of Burgundy, switched sides, an event that made French victory inevitable. Soon Paris was taken, then Normandy, and shortly thereafter Guienne. Though frail, Charles is credited with helping to create French absolutism by centralizing administration, including permanent and arbitrary taxation, and creating a standing army. Charles was also the victor in the Hundred Years' War. (NCE, 3, 501, s.v. Charles VII, King of France)

3. The civil wars in France during Mariana's lifetime (1536–1624) were the front line in the religious wars between Roman Catholics and Protes-

without home or fortune and with possessions lost—agreed to take up arms. They are destined either to destroy or be destroyed, choosing to end their misery by death, or, as conquerors, to plunder riches and power. To help achieve this goal, they cloaked their obstinacy with a veil of religion and their perversity with rectitude. Countless evils have ensued.

There is certainly little benefit in summoning procurators of the states to parliaments in Castile. Most of them are poorly equipped to manage affairs. They are men who are led by chance—insignificant men of venal disposition who keep nothing in view but their desire to gain the prince's favor and to benefit from public disaster. The temptations and threats of the courtiers, mixed with prayers and promises, would uproot and fell the cedars of Lebanon. It is beyond doubt and, as things now stand, sufficiently obvious that these men will never oppose the prince's wish that he should be in total command. It would be better if these parliaments were never held. They are an excuse for useless expenditures and widespread corruption. Be that as it may, here we are not discussing what is happening but rather what right reason demands. New taxes should not be imposed on subjects without their free consent—not by force, curses, or threats.

As Comineus also advises, the people should show themselves amenable and not resist the prince's wishes. Rather, as need arises, they should manfully come to the aid of the depleted treasury; but the prince should also afford a patient ear, listen to the people, and diligently consider whether their substance and means are up to bearing the new burden, or whether there may not be other solutions to the problem. The prince may have to be exhorted to moderate and responsible spending. This, I

---

tants. The unrest in France was also fomented by Francis I's creation of the *trésorier de l'épargne*, which was designed to facilitate the collection of taxes and provide needed revenue for warfare and a lavish court. Although the *trésorier de l'épargne* attempted to centralize all monetary activity, its purpose was never quite accomplished, and Francis continually searched for new sources of revenue. (NCE, 6, 27, s.v. Francis I, King of France)

understand, was occasionally attempted at earlier parliaments within the kingdom. The established principle, therefore, is that the prince is never permitted to oppress his subjects with new burdens without the consent of those concerned, at least of the leaders of the people and state.

What I said above confirms this point: The private goods of citizens are not at the disposal of the king. Thus, he must not take all or part of them without the approval of those who have the right to them. This is the pronouncement of legal experts: The king does not have the power to make a decision that results in loss of private goods unless the owners agree, nor may he seize any part of their property by planning and imposing a new tax. Why? Because the office of leader or director does not give him this power. Rather, because the king has the power from the state to receive specific income to maintain his original lifestyle, if he wishes these taxes to be increased, he would fulfill his duties by approaching those who originally decide on that specific income. It is their job to grant or deny what he seeks, as seems good to them, under the circumstances. Other countries may do things in different ways. In our country, this method is forbidden by the 1329 law that Alfonso XI,[4] King of Castile, granted to the people in the parliament of Madrid in response to petition 68: "Let no tax be imposed on the nation against the will of the people." Here is the law: "In addition, because the petitioners have requested that no extraordinary tax be imposed, either

---

4. Alfonso XI (1311–1350) of Castile and León, son of Ferdinand IV and Constance of Portugal, succeeded to the throne in 1312 and began his reign in 1325. During the reign of Alfonso XI, "Significant legislative work and judicial streamlining were carried out at the Cortes of Burgos in 1328 and at the Cortes of Segovia in 1347. In 1348, the Cortes meeting at Alcalá de Henares produced the very important *Ordenamiento de Alcalá de Henares*, which confirmed previous laws; set up new rules on matters of procedure, wills, contracts, and royal dealings with the nobility; and above all, established the order of precedence of the law then in force in Castile and León." (DMA, 7, 523, s.v. Law, Spanish)

publicly or privately, unless the people have been previously summoned into parliament and the tax has been approved by all of the procurators of the states. We reply to this request: We are pleased with it. We decree that it is to be done."

In the previously cited place, Philippus Comineus repeats these words in French—twice: "Therefore, to pursue my point, no king or prince on earth can demand, except by way of violence and tyranny, even one *maravedi* from his nation, if those designated to pay it are unwilling." A little later, in addition to the claim of tyranny, Comineus adds that a prince who would act contrary to this law would incur the penalty of excommunication. His source may be the sixth chapter of the *Bulla in Coena Domini*[5] that excommunicates anyone who imposes new taxes in his realm. At this point, some documents read: "Unless authorization has been granted for this purpose." Others read: "Except where it has been granted by right and law." Let others judge whether

---

5. A bull is an occasional letter issued by the Roman Pontiffs of their most important utterances. The quasi-official collection of bulls and briefs is known as the *Bullarium Romanum* and includes encyclicals, motu proprios, and other similar constitutions that possess just the same force, as sources of the canon law, as the decretals one would expect to find there. After the thirteenth century, due largely to the great codifying and systematizing work of Innocent III, bulls are commonly classified as either *tituli* or *mandamenta*. The *tituli* were for the most part acts of grace (*indulgentiae*), concessions of privileges, confirmations, decisions on points of doctrine or law, and so forth, whereas the *mandamenta* represented the ordinary correspondence of the Holy See. They were orders of the pope, commissions to conduct an inquiry or to reform abuses, letters written to communicate some important knowledge to invite the cooperation of temporal sovereigns, or to prescribe a line of conduct for clergy or laity. It is important to note that the decretals, upon which the structure of canon law was built, almost always took the form of lesser bulls, that is, simple letters or *mandamenta*. The first known *Bulla in Coena Domini*, containing the "Reserved Cases" of the Holy See, issued by Urban V in 1364, was a *mandamentum*. The range and scope of issues that this particular bull addressed grew over time and included such items as how to handle tyrannical princes, usury, and matters pertaining to coinage. (ERE, 2, 891–97, s.v. Bulls and Briefs)

kings who do otherwise are exempt from this excommunication. How can they be? Neither do they have the power to tax, nor has the additional right been given to them. Yet, because Comineus was a literary man, and not in sacred orders, what he affirmed in such a statement depended upon the authority of the theologians of that time who were agreed on this point.

I personally add that not only any prince who acts this way in regard to taxes is guilty of this crime and punishment but also any prince who would fraudulently establish a monopoly without the consent of the people. It is equally fraudulent under another name, as is stealing the possessions of one's subjects to sell things for a higher price than is fair without authorization. In fact, for some years the prince has established some monopolies on lotteries, corrosive sublimate, and salt. I do not call these monopolies into question. Rather, I consider them prudently established and concerning the uprightness and the fidelity of the prince, one must believe that he has done nothing that goes beyond right reason and the laws. However, the point is, that as monopolies do not differ from taxes, caution in establishing them legally and in demanding popular consent should be no less. An example will make the point clearer. In Castile, there has frequently been talk of publicly imposing a tax on flour. Until now, the people have resisted it with difficulty, but if it were permissible for the king to buy up all the grain in the land to monopolize it and to sell it at a higher price, then it would be superfluous and meaningless to have the imposition of taxes depend upon the will of the people. In such a case, the king has the freedom to gain whatever he wishes through a monopoly that yields the same or even greater advantages than taxes. From what has been said, the point is firmly established that, if a king is not permitted to demand new taxes, he cannot even set up monopolies for merchandise without the consultation and approval of the people concerned.

3

CAN THE KING DEBASE MONEY BY CHANGING ITS WEIGHT OR QUALITY WITHOUT CONSULTING THE PEOPLE?

Two things are clear. First, the king may change at will the form and engraving of money—provided that he does not diminish its value. That is the way I interpret the legal experts who grant the king the power to change money. The king owns the mints and administers them, and under the heading of "Regalia" in the *Novellas constitutiones*, money is listed among the other royal prerogatives. Therefore, without any loss to his subjects, he determines the method for minting money as he pleases. Second, we grant the king the authority to debase money without the people's consent in the pressing circumstances of war or siege—provided that the debasement is not extended beyond the time of need and that when peace has been restored he faithfully makes satisfaction to those who suffered loss.

In a very harsh winter, Frederick Augustus II[1] was holding Faenza under siege. Those under siege were powerless. The siege

---

1. Frederick Augustus II (1194–1250), son of Emperor Henry VI and Constance, daughter of Roger VI of Sicily, succeeded to the throne in 1220. Frederick's reign united the Hohenstaufen claims to the imperial throne

was protracted, and money was lacking for salaries. He ordered money struck from leather, with his image on one side and the imperial eagle on the other, and each coin had the value of a gold coin. He did this on his own, without consultation with the people of the empire. The salvific plan brought about the conclusion of the affair. With his forces reassured by this device, he took over the city. When the war was over, he replaced the leather money with just as many golden coins. Collenucius[2] relates this occurrence in the fourth book of his *History of Naples*. In France as well, money was struck on occasion from leather and decorated with a small silver key. Budelius,[3] in the first book of

---

and his mother's claim to rule the Kingdom of Sicily. In 1220, Frederick descended into Italy to claim his mother's territory. At this time, Honorius III placed the imperial crown upon his head, while Frederick pledged anew to take up the cross. However, unrest in the Kingdom of Sicily increased the difficulty in establishing his rule there, which took five years to resolve. Mariana's reference to the events surrounding Frederick's siege of the northern Italian city of Faenza took place early in the Italian invasion. Of all the heirs of Charlemagne, it is said that Frederick II came closest to sharing his vision. With Frederick's death, the Holy Roman Empire lost most of its spirit and vitality. (NCE, 6, 86–87, s.v. Frederick II, Roman Emperor)

2. Pandolfo Collenuccio (1444–1504), historian, poet, scientist, and statesman, studied law at Padua and then entered the service of the Sforza at Pesaro. He was an accomplished diplomat and carried out numerous missions for his patrons, until he was expelled from Pesaro by his lord, Giovanni Sforza. Collenuccio's great reputation as a lawyer, man of letters, and skillful diplomat brought him into contact with Lorenzo the Magnificent, Ercole I d'Este, the Emperor Maximilian, and Pope Alexander VI. Collenuccio wrote a history of Naples (*Compendio della historie del regno di Napoli*), Latin and Italian poems, and made the translation *Anfitrione* of the comedy of Plautus. (NCIRE, 257, s.v. Collenuccio, Pandolfo)

3. René Budel was born in Ruremonde in 1530. His death date, however, is unknown. He was a lawyer and worked as a diplomat in the service of the Electors of Cologne and the Dukes of Bayern who appointed him as the mint-master in the Duchy of Westfalen. His work, *De Monetis et Re nummaria libri duos: his accesserunt tractatus varii atque utiles tam veterum quam neotericorum authorum*, which Mariana cites, appeared in Cologne in 1591. The first book treats the art of money stamping, while the second

his *On Money* (chap. 1, no. 34), recalls that money was made from paper when Leiden in Holland was under siege in 1574. These facts are undisputed.

However, the question is this: Can a prince in every case solve his fiscal problems on his own authority and debase his kingdom's money by diminishing its weight or its quality? Certainly the common opinion of legal experts agrees with that of Hostiensius,[4] expressed in his *De censibus* in the paragraph *Ex quibus*. Among these experts are Innocent[5] and Panormitanus

---

evaluates legal questions, which earlier scholars had divided into strict compartments, tied up with a monetary system. (Nbg, 7–8, 726, s.v. Budel or Budelius, René)

4. Hostiensius (1200–1271), also known as Henry of Segusio or Enrico Bartolomei, was a cardinal and canonist whose writings exerted great influence on canon law in the thirteenth century and beyond. He was not only one of the most famous decretalists, he was also a competent diplomat. Innocent IV appointed him archbishop of Embrun. His important work, the *Lectura in quinque libros decretalium*, is a commentary upon all of Gregory IX's decretals. The *Lectura*, along with his *Summa "Copiosa,"* both written early in his career when he taught in Paris, synthesized Roman and canon law and thus accomplished a summary of the *utrumque ius*. These treatises became the stock-in-trade of canonists until well into the seventeenth century. (NCE, 7, 170–71, s.v. Hostiensis [Henry of Segusio])

5. Pope Innocent III (1160/61–1216), whose papacy began in 1198, embodies better than any other medieval papal representative the belief that the pope was the true Vicar of Christ on earth. He brought into clear relief the exclusively legal function of the pope as the successor of Peter, at the same time making precise the definition of Petrine powers as vicarious powers of Christ himself. In one of his consecration sermons, Innocent declared that he was less than God but greater than man, standing as it were in the middle. The exercise of the papal plenitude of power was the hallmark of his papacy. His pontificate was characterized by a large legislative output; more than six thousand letters are extant of which many were decretals. This enormous corpus stimulated canonistic scholarship at Bologna and led to a number of canonical collections in his pontificate. As the administrator of the Roman Curia, Innocent created a sound, orderly financial administration: His pontificate was one of only a few that did not experience financial difficulties. (NCE, 7, 521–24, s.v. Innocent III, Pope)

who, in the fourth chapter of *De iureiurando*, maintains that a prince may not do this without the consent of his subjects.

One concludes, therefore, that if the king is the director—not the master—of the private possessions of his subjects, he will not be able to take away arbitrarily any part of their possessions for this or any other reason or any ploy. Such seizure occurs whenever money is debased: For what is declared to be more is worth less. Thus, if a prince is not empowered to levy taxes on unwilling subjects and cannot set up monopolies for merchandise, he is not empowered to make fresh profit from debased money. These strategies aim at the same thing: cleaning out the pockets of the people and piling up money in the provincial treasury. Do not be taken in by the smoke and mirrors by which metal is given a greater value than it has by nature and in common estimation. Of course this does not happen without common injury. When blood is let by whatever device or strategy, the body will certainly be debilitated and wasted. In the same way, a prince cannot profit without the suffering and groans of his subjects. As Plato maintained, one man's profit is another's loss.[6] No one can abrogate by any means these fundamental laws of nature. In chapter 5 of *De iureiurando*, I find that Innocent III judges to be invalid the oath by which James the Conqueror,[7] King of

---

6. Plato (428/427–349/348 BC), student and devoted follower of Socrates, founded his own philosophical school in Athens called the Academy after Socrates' death in 399. Through the Academy, Plato intended not only to promote philosophy and science but also to affect politics from a distance. He is credited with composing twenty-eight dialogues, of which modern scholars generally agree that only twenty-four are probably authentic. Mariana is likely referring here to Plato's discussion of plutocracy in the *Republic* (VIII.550c–555b).

7. James I (1208–1276), also known as James the Conqueror, succeeded to the throne in 1213. During his youth, he was a ward of Pope Innocent III. James used the political resources of Aragón-Catalonia to conquer the Muslim kingdom of Valencia and the Balearics. By encouraging the communes, the newly developing mendicant orders, and the universities,

Aragón, bound himself for a considerable time to preserve the debased money that his father, Peter II,[8] had minted. Among other reasons for this opinion is the fact that the consent of the people was lacking. Both Innocent and Panormitanus support this view. They confirm that a prince cannot establish anything that would cause injury to the people. We call it an injury when anything is taken from a person's fortune.

Indeed, I do not know how those who do these things can avoid the excommunication and censure pronounced for all ages by the *Bulla in Coena Domini*, because it applies to monopolies. All such schemes, under any pretense, aim at the same thing: to weigh the people down with new burdens and to amass money. This is not permissible, for if anyone maintains that our kings were granted this power long ago by the people's carelessness and

---

James was instrumental in transforming a feudally organized society into a proto-kingdom. Though he endowed numerous churches and introduced religious orders on a large scale, he withheld a disproportionate share of the tithes, repudiated his wife despite papal exhortations to the contrary, and persisted in a life of public adultery. (NCE, 7, 806, s.v. James I, King of Aragón)

8. Peter II (1174–1213), son of Alfonso II, succeeded to the throne of Aragón-Catalonia in 1196 and reigned until his death on the battlefield of Muret in 1213. In 1204, he married Mary, lady of Montpellier, and a few months later had himself crowned at Rome by Pope Innocent III, to whom he agreed to pay an annual tribute. This event increased his prestige among the Christian monarchs, and led quite naturally to his ambitious role in the united crusading army that defeated the Almohuds at Las Navas de Tolosa in 1212. Like his father, Peter's opulent and extravagant lifestyle led him to turn compensations for the maintenance of monetary stability and peace into territorial subsidies, but, in the process, there was a terrible abuse of precedents and customs. As a result, in 1205 the Catalonian barons tried unsuccessfully to impose a charter on Peter, who countered desperately by imposing a money-tax (ostensibly a compensation for maintaining stable coinage) not only on Catalonia (for the second time in his reign) but also, for the first time ever, on Aragón. (DMA, 1, 408–21, s.v. Aragón, Crown of [1137–1479])

indulgence, I find no trace of this custom or permission. Rather, I find that the laws concerning money of both the Catholic King[9] and Philip,[10] his great-grandson, were always passed in the nation's parliaments.

---

9. The title "Catholic King" or "Catholic rulers" refers either in the singular, as in this instance, to Ferdinand II of Aragón (1452–1516), son of John II of Aragón and Johanna Enríquez or, in the plural, to Ferdinand II of Aragón and Isabella (1451–1504), daughter of John II of Castile and Isabella of Portugal.

10. Philip II (1527–1598), son of Charles I of Spain (the Emperor Charles V) and Isabella of Portugal, began his reign in 1543 as regent in Spain during his father's absence in Germany. In 1556, Philip succeeded to the throne, which included the crown of Castile with Navarre and the Indies, the crown of Aragón-Catalonia with Sardinia, and the crown of Sicily—a veritable world empire. However, financial difficulties forced him to settle in Spain, impose his authority, and withdraw from the widespread commitments of his father. He distrusted subordinates and governed as an absolute monarch, but he always respected the autonomous status of the constituent kingdoms. (NCE, 11, 272–73, s.v. Philip II, King of Spain)

4

THE TWOFOLD VALUE
OF MONEY

Money has a twofold value. One is intrinsic and natural and comes from its type of metal and its weight, to which may be added the cost for labor and equipment in minting. The other is called the legal value and is extrinsic, inasmuch as it is established by the law of the prince, who has the right to prescribe the worth of money as well as of other goods. In a well-constituted republic, it should be the care of those who are in control of such matters to see that these two values are equal and do not differ, for just as in the case of other goods, it would be unjust for something to be appraised at ten when it is worth five in itself and in common estimation, so the same thing holds for money if the legal value goes astray. This point is treated by Budelius in the first book of his *On Money* (chap. 1, no. 7), among other scholars, and they commonly consider anyone who thinks otherwise ridiculous and childish. If it is permissible to separate these values, let them mint money from leather, from paper, from lead, as we know was done in strained circumstances. The reckoning would be the same, and the cost for manufacturing less than if money were made of bronze.

I do not think that a king should produce money at his own expense, but I think it fair that some value be added to the worth of the metal in consideration of the labor of minting and of the overall monetary ministry. It would not be out of place if some small profit accrued to a prince from this function as a sign of his sovereignty and his prerogative. This opinion was ratified in the law, promulgated in Madrid in 1566,[1] concerning the making of silver coins (*cuartillos*). In the fifth chapter of his *De iureiurando*, Innocent III implies this practice even if he does not mention it explicitly. I, however, maintain that these two values must be diligently and accurately kept equal. This same conviction may be gathered from Aristotle's *Politics* (bk. 1, chap. 6)[2] where he says that it was originally taken for granted that men would exchange one thing for another. By common opinion, it seemed best to exchange merchandise for iron and silver, to avoid expense, and to ease the aggravation of transporting long distances wares that were heavy and cumbersome for both parties. Thus, a sheep was exchanged for so many pounds of brass, a horse for so many pounds of gold. It was difficult to weigh metal consistently. Public authority undertook to see to it that parts of the metal were marked with their weight to expedite commerce. This was the first and legitimate use of money, though time and evil produced other devices and deceptions that are certainly at odds with ancient and wholesome usage.

As our own laws tell us, our countrymen clearly decided that the two values be kept equal. Indeed, gold and silver are clear instances of this equality. Sixty-seven silver coins are made from 8 ounces of silver, called a *mark*, while the same weight of natural

---

1. The monetary policy of Philip II originated in the parliamentary assembly of Madrid in 1566. The laws of 1497 and 1566 concern nearly all of the various monetary species.

2. Mariana's reference to chapter 6 of book 1 is inaccurate. Aristotle addresses the art of acquisition (or exchange) in book 1, chapter 9 of the *Politics*.

silver is exchanged for 65 silver coins, both in accordance with the prescripts of law. Thus, only 2 silver coins are added for the work involved in minting. Each silver coin is equivalent to 34 *maravedis*, while the same weight of natural silver is valued at about 33 *maravedis*. What about gold? Sixty-eight gold coins, called *coronas*, are struck from 8 ounces of gold. Natural gold is worth about the same amount. Copper money is valued in the same way, but in this case it seems more difficult to reconcile the legal value with the natural value.

According to the law promulgated in Medina del Campo in 1497, the Catholic Kings ordained that 8 ounces of copper, mixed with 7 grains of silver (about the weight of 1½ silver coins), would make 96 *maravedis*. The silver was worth more than 51 *maravedis*. The 8 ounces of copper and the cost of labor approximate the other 44 *maravedis* in value. In this way, the legal value is easily reconciled with the value of the metal and the labor.

Then in 1566, Philip II, King of Spain, abrogated the previous law and established that 4 grains of silver—the weight of 1 silver coin—were to be mixed with 8 ounces of copper. From this mixture, 110 *maravedis* were to be minted. In so doing, he took away more than half of the silver from the quality of the metal, and added 14 *maravedis* to the old value. He was, I think, considering the expense of minting, which doubtless had doubled with time, as well as made a profit from his supervision. Led on by this modest and slender hope, many men—after they had been authorized by the king to produce this money—made an immense profit. Consequently, as in past years, this business was considered especially lucrative. Yet the two values of money were not unreconciled in this approach, because the value of silver was mixed in with the 8 ounces of copper, and one must include both the price of copper and of production, both of which were estimated by at least two other silver coins. Moreover, debased money, which we call *blancas*, valued at half a *maravedi*, was being frequently minted and was a source of much greater vexation and nuisance.

At this time, no silver was mixed with copper in copper money, and 8 ounces of copper yielded 280 *maravedis*. The entire cost for stamping did not exceed a silver coin. Copper was selling at 46 *maravedis*. The cost of stamping and the value of the metal thus came to 80 *maravedis*. The profit was therefore 200 *maravedis* on each *mark* because the legal value of this money exceeded the intrinsic and natural value of the metal. The great danger that this fact presents to the state needs explanation. First, as indicated above, it is inconsistent with the nature and original concept of money. How, then, can anyone be stopped from debasing money in like circumstances, when enticed by the hope of gigantic profit? Finally, these values will adjust in business, as people are reluctant to give and take money that is worth more than its natural value. Fictions and frauds, once discovered, quickly collapse, and a prince who opposes the people will accomplish nothing. Would he be able to insist that rough sackcloth be sold for the cost of silken velvet, or that woolen clothing be sold for cloth of gold? Clearly, he could not. Try as he might, he could not justly make such a practice legal.

The French kings frequently devalued the *solidus*, and our silver coins were immediately valued higher than before. What was previously worth 4 *solidi*, when we were dwelling in France, became worth 7 or 8 *solidi*. If the legal value of debased money does not decrease, surely all merchandise will sell at a higher price, in proportion to the debasement of the quality or the weight of the money. The process is inevitable. As a result, the price of goods adjusts and money is less valuable than it previously and properly was.

5

THE FOUNDATIONS OF COMMERCE: MONEY, WEIGHTS, AND MEASURES

Weights, measures, and money are, of course, the foundations of commerce upon which rests the entire structure of trade. Most things are sold by weight and measure—but everything is sold by money. Everyone wants the foundations of buildings to remain firm and secure, and the same holds true for weights, measures, and money. They cannot be changed without danger and harm to commerce.

The ancients understood this. One of their major concerns was to preserve a specimen of all these things in their holy temples so that no one might rashly falsify them. Fannius[1] bears witness to this fact in his *De ponderibus et mensuris*, and a law of Justinian

---

1. It is not entirely clear who Mariana has in mind with the reference to Fannius. Fannius was a common Plebeian nomen, attested historically from the beginning of the second century BC. Perhaps, Mariana is referring to Fannius, the Plebian aedile and mint master in 86 BC, who went on to become a judge and later (in 80) the praetor and chairman of the court for murder cases. (BNP, 5, 350–52, s.v. Fannius)

Augustus[2] concerning this tradition is extant (*Authent. De collatoribus* coll. 9). In Leviticus (27:25) we read: "Every valuation shall be according to the *shekel* of the sanctuary." Some conclude that the Jews were accustomed to keep a *shekel* weighing 4 *drachmas* of silver in the sanctuary to ensure easy recourse to a legitimate *shekel*, so that no one would dare to falsify it by tampering with its quality and weight. It was so important to maintain standards that no amount of care was considered superfluous. Even Thomas Aquinas warns (*De regim. Principum*, bk. 2, chap. 14)[3] that money should not be altered rashly or at the whim of

---

2. The Roman Emperor Justinian (527–565 AD) was born c. 482 of Thracian-Illyrian origins as the son of a farmer, with the Latin name Petrus Sabatius in Bederiana by Tauresium. Justinian owed his rise to Iustinus I, his mother's brother. When his uncle came to power in 518, he adopted Justinian and crowned him co-emperor in 527, after which Justinian's name became Justinian Augustus. Justinian's most important achievement, which stood the test of time, was the compilation of the *Corpus iuris civilis*. In 528, Justinian charged a commission with collecting all imperial laws. The commission completed its task in 534. In 533, the *Institutiones*, an elementary legal treatise, became law, and that same year, the *Digest*, the codification of classical jurisprudence, was promulgated. The laws made after 534, the *Novellae*, were not officially sanctioned as Justinian had intended; they were passed down in private compilations. (BNP, 6, 1136–39, s.v. Iustinianus; and DMA, 7, 418–25, s.v. Law, Civil—*CORPUS IURIS*, Revival and Spread)

3. Even though Thomas Aquinas (1225–1274) left behind no systematic treatment of politics, his treatise *De regimine principum*, which was compiled for the education of a prince and followed the pattern of similar handbooks in the Middle Ages, was widely read in its day and considered to be a valuable source of his political theory. The commentaries on Aristotle's *Ethics* and *Politics* were also valuable sources of information for Thomas's understanding of politics. By far, however, the most important material is to be found in his philosophical and theological works, from the commentary on Peter Lombard's *Sentences* to the great *Summae*. "But," as A. P. D'Entrèves cautions, Thomas's treatment of politics "is scattered and fragmentary, and the greatest care must be taken in severing such fragments from the general frame in which they fit and from which they derive their significance" (p. viii). See *Aquinas: Selected Political Writings*, ed. A. P. D'Entrèves, trans. J. G. Dawson (Oxford: Basil Blackwell, 1974), vii–xxxiii.

a prince. The recent change in the liquid measure in Castile, by which new tribute was exacted on wine and oil—not without protest—is reprehensible. In addition to other inconveniences, there is a problem adjusting the old measure to the new, and further confusion in our dealings with others. Those who are in power seem less educated than the people because they pay no attention to the disturbances and evils frequently caused by their decisions, both in our nation and beyond. Obviously, debasing money will profit the king, and we have proof that the ancients were frequently led into fraud by that hope and that these same men soon became aware of the disadvantages of their decisions. To remedy these ills, new and greater ills were needed: The situation is like giving a drink at the wrong time to a sick man. At first, it refreshes him but later aggravates the causes of his illness and increases his fever. The clear fact is that great care was once taken that these foundations of human existence be not disturbed. In my *De ponderibus et mensuris*[4] (chap. 8), I explained that the Roman ounce remained unchanged for many centuries and that it is the same as ours. The same should be true of the other weights. Our weights should not differ from those of the ancients.

---

4. Juan de Mariana, *De ponderibus et mensuris* (Toledo: T. Gusmanium, 1599).

6

MONEY HAS FREQUENTLY BEEN ALTERED

A widespread opinion among the Jews was that the money, measures, and weights of the sanctuary were twice as great as the common ones: the *bathum*, *gomor*, *shekel*, and all the rest. They thought this way because their special effort to preserve the weights and measures in the sanctuary could not prevent the people from diminishing the common ones and, under some conditions, making them less than half. Thus, different passages in ancient writers that vary in specifics or are at odds with sacred letters may be reconciled.

We know—and Pliny[1] (bk. 33, chap. 3) testifies to this fact— that in ancient Rome, the *as* (a copper coin with the value of 4

---

1. Pliny the Elder (4–79 AD), Gaius Plinius Secundus, prominent Roman equestrian, commander of the fleet at Misenum, and uncle of Pliny the Younger was best known as the author of the 37-volume *Naturalis Historia*, an encyclopedia of all contemporary knowledge—animal, vegetable, mineral, and human. Pliny's summation of universal knowledge in the *Naturalis Historia* became a model for later writers such as Iulius Solinus and Isidorus and attained a position of enormous cultural and intellectual influence in the medieval west. (OCD, 1197–98, s.v. Pliny the Elder)

of our current *maravedis*), under the pressure of the First Punic War,[2] was debased to 2 ounces, which they called a sextantarian *as*,[3] which weighed about ⅙ of a pound—then 12 ounces, like the Italian and French *pound* today. Thereafter, under pressure during the war with Hannibal,[4] the Romans reduced the *as* to an ounce, $\frac{1}{12}$ of the previous *asses*, and finally the reduction in weight reached half an ounce. The *denarius*, with a value of 40 *maravedis*, was initially minted from pure silver. Then under Drusus, the Tribune of the Plebs,[5] was mixed with an eighth

---

2. The First Punic War lasted from 264 to 241 BC. This war was one of three in which Rome successfully fought Carthage for dominance in the western Mediterranean. The scene of the first campaigns was Sicily. In 263, the Romans won a victory that resulted in Hieron II, tyrant of Syracuse, entering into alliance with Rome. In 262, the Romans won Segesta and Agrigentum but realized that to drive the Carthaginians out of Sicily they needed to overcome the latters' naval superiority. They were successful in 260, but the situation in Sicily remained indecisive. Thus, the Romans sent a force to Africa in 256 whose efforts were ultimately successful. The Carthaginians evacuated Sicily, which became the first Roman province, and had to pay an indemnity of 3,200 talents. Thus, at the end of the First Punic War, Carthage was in dire financial straits and turned to Spain to recoup wealth and manpower. (OCD, 1277–78, s.v. Punic Wars)

3. *Sextantarius*, or containing a sextans, is a sixth part of a measure.

4. Hannibal's (247–182 BC) attack on Rome's Spanish ally Saguntum in 219 precipitated the Second Punic War (218–202 BC). Hannibal intercepted Roman dispatches sent to Spain and Africa and then invaded northern Italy. He reached Italy in 218 and ultimately engaged the Roman army head on at Cannae in 216. Rome suffered a bloody defeat there but later managed to cut off Hannibal's reinforcements from Spain. After the capture of Syracuse in 211 the tide began to turn for Rome. The war ended in 202 with the final defeat of Carthage who had to pay an annual indemnity of 10,000 talents. Needless to say, the war seriously taxed Roman financial resources. (OCD, 665–66, s.v. Hannibal)

5. Tribunes were the officers of the people (plebs), first created in 500–450 BC. These officers were magistrates who were themselves plebian and of free birth. The original number of the tribunes was two; by 449 it had risen to ten. The tribunes were charged with the defense of the persons and property of the plebians. Their power derived not from statute initially but

part of copper and its previous purity was changed, as Pliny indicates in the same passage. In subsequent years, more copper was added. Actually, not a few *denarii* are being unearthed in our time that contain much less silver and are of less purity because of the greater weight of copper added—more than a third. Likewise, gold money of outstanding purity and weighing 2 *drachmas* was minted during the reigns of the first emperors. At that time they were minted from 6 ounces of gold and were called *solidi*. They weighed about the same as our *castellano*. A law of Emperor Justinian concerning *solidi* can be found under the heading *De susceptoribus, praepositis et arcariis*, and begins with "Quotiescumque."[6] Commenting on the freedom to innovate in one of his prologues, the ancient poet, Plautus,[7] seems to suggest

---

from the oath sworn by the plebians to guarantee the tribunes' inviolability (*sacrosanctitas*). Elected by the plebian assembly and exercising their power within the precincts of the city, the tribunes could summon the people to assembly and elicit resolutions. They asserted a right of enforcing the decrees of the people and their own rights; in subsequent years, they possessed a right of veto against any act performed by a magistrate. In time, however, the tribunes became indistinguishable from magistrates of the state and beyond that became active in the pursuit of the people's interest, popular sovereignty, and public accountability. Mariana's reference to Drusus may be to Marcus Livius Drusus, tribune of the plebs in 122 BC and a supporter of the aristocracy against C. Gracchus. (BNP, 4, 726–727, s.v. Drusus; and OCD, 1549–50, s.v. Tribuni Plebis [or Plebi])

6. This subject is treated in a law found in the *Codex repetitae praelectionis* (12 books, ca. 534 AD), a smaller collection of laws contained within the *Codex Iustinianus*. The law itself dates from the year 367 and is located within the *Corpus iuris civilis* (Book III; *Codex repetitae praelectionis* X 72, 5). (DNP, 8, 1023–27, s.v. Novellae)

7. Titus Maccius Plautus (250–184 BC) is the first Roman comic playwright. He is the author of *fabulae palliate* between c. 205 and 184 BC, and his plays are the earliest Latin works to have survived intact. While some ancient authorities credit him with having written 130 plays, Varro drew up a list of 21 plays that were generally agreed to be by Plautus, and there is little doubt that these are the 21 carried over into modern editions. Nearly all of Plautus' plays are thought to be adaptations of Greek New

the Roman view of debasing money when he says, "Those who use old wine I consider wise. For the new comedies produced these days are much worse than the new coins."

Money still in existence today indicates how frequently the Romans changed the value of their money. The same thing has taken place in all countries within recent memory. Princes, with or without their subjects' consent, have frequently debased coins in quality or by subtracting from their weight. The search for examples in other countries is superfluous when domestic ones are at hand in abundance.

The history of Alfonso XI, the King of Castile (chap. 14) affirmed that money was altered by King Ferdinand the Holy[8] and

---

Comedy with plots portraying love affairs, confusion of identities, and misunderstandings. However, it should also be noted that "he adapted his models with considerable freedom and wrote plays that are in several respects quite different from anything we know of New Comedy. There is a large increase in the musical element. The roles of stock characters such as the parasite appear to have been considerably expanded. Consistency of characterization and plot development are cheerfully sacrificed for the sake of an immediate effect. The humour resides less in the irony of the situation than in jokes and puns. There are 'metatheatrical' references to the audience and to the progress of the play, or explicit reminders that the play is set in Greece. Above all, there is a constant display of verbal fireworks, with alliteration, wordplays, unexpected personifications, and riddling expressions." Plautus was well known in Renaissance Italy, particularly after the rediscovery of twelve plays in a manuscript found in Germany in 1429, and his plays were performed and imitated all over Europe until the seventeenth century but more sporadically thereafter. The lines that Mariana quotes came from the prologue to *Casina*, verses 5, 9, and 10. (OCD, 1194–96, s.v. Plautus [Titus Maccius Plautus])

8. Ferdinand III of Castile (1198–1252) succeeded to the throne in 1217, and is remembered for uniting Castile and León and reducing Muslim power in Andalusia to the kingdom of Granada. Ferdinand was born of the ill-fated union of Alfonso IX of León and Berengaria, daughter of Alfonso VIII of Castile. He succeeded to the Castilian crown after his mother, who had inherited it upon the premature death of her brother Henry I, had abdicated. His father opposed his son's accession to the throne but was unsuccessful in blocking it. Tolerant toward the Jews and Muslims who came under

by his son Alfonso the Wise,[9] as well as by Sancho the Brave,[10] by his son Ferdinand,[11] and by his grandson Alfonso XI. Therefore, during the reign of these five kings, which was sufficiently long, money enjoyed no stability; it was constantly changed and

---

his authority, Ferdinand strove to re-Christianize the conquered peoples through the new mendicant orders. He advanced legal studies through his promotion of the University of Salamanca. Furthermore, by centralizing the administration of his two kingdoms, he initiated the compilation of a uniform code of laws, a project completed by his successor, Alfonso the Wise. (NCE, 5, 886–887, s.v. Ferdinand III, King of Castile, St.)

9. Alfonso X of Castile (1221–1284) was the son of Ferdinand III and Beatrice of Suabia and was king of Castile and León (1252–1284). He faced almost insurmountable social, economic, and political crises. Some of these problems were of his own making and others he inherited from his father. Alfonso's reign was, with the exception of his patronage of letters and his legal program (which was not accepted until a century later), a failure. During his reign, Spanish culture and literature reached one of its high-water marks. He established schools in Seville, Murcia, and Toledo, in which Christians, Muslims, and Jews cultivated the arts and sciences. He also actively continued and contributed to the famous school of translators founded at Toledo in the twelfth century by Archbishop Raimundo (1130–1150). (NCE, 1, 311, s.v. Alfonso X, King of Castile)

10. Sancho IV of Castile and León (1258–1295) succeeded to the throne in 1284 against his father's strong protestations to the contrary. His marriage to his cousin, María de Molina, was within the forbidden degrees of consanguinity. The pope's reluctance to accept their union cast a shadow over the legitimacy of his line. Moreover, during the early years of his reign, Sancho IV came under the influence and control of Lope Díaz de Haro, lord of Vizcaya, who controlled the military and financial life of Castile. When the Castilian nobility revolted as a result of the spoils of the kingdom being monopolized by the Haro family, Sancho followed the sage advice of the king of Portugal to assassinate Lope Díaz. However, in the wake of this event, several conspiracies and revolts followed one after another. With the exception of some minor victories over the Muslims, Sancho had little to show but a realm divided by internal conflict and the nobility of Castile often allied to Granada against their own king. (DMA, 3, 134, s.v. Castile)

11. Ferdinand IV of Castile and León (1285–1312) was still a minor when his father died in 1295. Once again, Castile sank into anarchy. The prominent families fought each other for the regency. Several claimants

debased. Remarkably, Peter,[12] the king of Castile and the son of
the last Alfonso does not seem to have debased the currency. I
suspect that, rather inhibited by the inconveniences caused by
the adulteration of money when his father was in power, he did
not follow Alfonso's example and was careful to mint proper
money. This is attested by the money minted under his name.
His brother Henry II,[13] ridden by debt that he owed to his com-

---

sought the throne. Armies from Aragón and Portugal entered Castilian territory with the intention of setting the son of Ferdinand de la Cerda over a
dismembered kingdom. It was only because of the energy and determination
of the queen mother, María de Molina, who rallied the urban centers and
their militias to the cause of her son, that the realm survived. The leagues
of towns became the protectors of the boy king. Even so, Ferdinand IV
could claim his throne in 1301 only after major concessions to his enemies.
His troubled reign came to an end in 1312, leaving yet another child who
was just over a year old, Alfonso XI, to assume the throne in time. (DMA,
3, 134, s.v. Castile)

12. Peter I of Castile and León (1334–1369) succeeded to the throne
in 1350 following his father's death at Gibraltar. Peter began his rule with
Castile devastated by the plague and by a severe economic and social
crisis. He made an effort to solve some of these problems at a meeting of
the cortes in Valladolid in 1351. His economic and political objective—to
destroy the power of the high nobility, to make the king supreme in Castile,
to make Castile supreme in Spain—was carried out with the support of
the newly university-trained elite and the Jews. During the latter half of
his reign, a protracted civil war broke out between Castile and Aragón.
Peter's opposition sought an alliance with and the support of Charles V of
France, in addition Bertrand du Guesclin and his mercenary companies
were hired to kill Peter. In response, Peter enlisted English support and
Edward of Wales entered Spain and, joining forces with Peter, defeated
their enemies in 1367. However, when Peter could not fulfill his promises
to the English, he was left alone, an easy target for the angry nobility and
the French. Eventually, Peter was murdered in a plot by Du Guesclin and
Henry II of Castile and León in 1369. (DMA, 3, 136–37, s.v. Castile; BU,
12, 172–76, s.v. DUGUESCLIN [Bertrand])

13. Henry II of Castile and León (1333–1379) succeeded to the throne
in 1369. Henry began his reign under attack by Peter's supporters and by
a coalition of Portugal, Navarre, Aragón, and Granada. In addition, to a

panions and assistants in exchange for winning the kingdom and burdened with larger illegal debts for the future had recourse to the same remedy. He minted two types of money: *reales* (silver coins) worth 3 *maravedis*, and *cruzados* worth 1 *maravedi*, as the chronicles (chap. 10) for the fourth year of his reign testify.

Serious inconveniences arose from this contrivance, but his successors were not afraid to follow his example. To pay Alencastre,[14] the duke of a rival kingdom, the money agreed upon in a peace treaty, John I[15] devised a new coin by the name of *blanca*, worth 1 *maravedi*, and shortly thereafter he decreed that the *blanca*, almost halved in value, be evaluated at only 6 *dineros* called *novenes*. This took place in the parliaments of Burgos in 1387. The right to devalue money by diminishing quality and increasing value continued into the reign of Henry IV.[16] These

---

large extent he owed the throne to the aid received from the nobility and now the time had come to pay his debt. His huge grants to the aristocracy weakened the financial foundations of the realm and led to the formation of a powerful and extremely wealthy oligarchy. (DMA, 3, 137, s.v. Castile)

14. The duke of Lancaster (John of Gaunt, second son of Edward III of England) laid claim to the throne through his marriage to Constance, the daughter of Peter I of Castile.

15. John I of Castile and León (1358–1390) succeeded to the throne in 1379. He made every effort to check the excesses of the nobility and to centralize royal authority. His reforms of the financial and administrative bodies—the Royal Council, audiencia, and leagues of towns—and the prominence of the cortes were worthy accomplishments but were ultimately overshadowed by his failure in Portugal. John's monetary reforms should be placed within the broader context of the 1387 monetary reform in the parliament of Burgos and the economic effect of the Hundred Years' War on Europe generally. When Ferdinand I of Portugal died in 1383, John I claimed the throne through his wife, Beatriz of Portugal, but his ambitions were thwarted by the resistance of the Portuguese and their election of a new king, John of Avis. (DMA, 3, 137, s.v. Castile)

16. Henry IV of Castile and León (1425–1474) succeeded to the throne in 1454. Henry, a complex and tragic figure, was vilified by the supporters of his half-sister Isabella and dominated from early youth by a succession of favorites, especially the greedy John Pacheco, marquis of Villena. The

were the most unsettled of times and, although the historians of the period do not say so, this fact is patently clear from the fluctuations in the value of silver, for when Alfonso XI was king of Castile, 8 ounces of silver were worth 125 *maravedis*. During the reign of Henry II, a silver *real* was worth 3 *maravedis* and, consequently, a *mark*[17] was worth 400 *maravedis*. Under John I, Henry's son, it went up to 250 *maravedis*; a silver coin was worth 4 *maravedis*; a gold coin was worth 50 *maravedis* or 12 silver coins. Such is found in the 1388 parliament of Burgos (Law 1). Under Henry III,[18] his successor, the value reached 480 or even 500 *maravedis*. Indeed, at the end of his reign and the beginning of John II's,[19] the value increased to 1000 *maravedis*. Finally, in the

---

first half of his reign evidences a desire for reform, indicated by judicious policies carried out either by the king or his advisors. However, his war policies against Granada, a war of attrition rather than the frontal attack called for by the aristocracy, and Henry's dependence on obscure nobles, precipitated a revolt of the nobility in 1464 and, for all practical purposes, the decline of royal influence. (DMA, 3, 138, s.v. Castile)

17. That is, 8 ounces of silver.

18. Henry III of Castile and León (1379–1406) succeeded to the throne in 1390. He reached his majority in 1393. Although set back by ill health, he achieved some important gains. During Henry's reign, Castile began its expansion in the Atlantic with the conquest of the Canary Islands early in the fifteenth century, and the high nobility stayed relatively quiet and content during this time. When Henry died in 1406, his programs were still in their infancy and had not yet been consolidated. (DMA, 3, 137–38, s.v. Castile)

19. John II of Castile and León (1405–1454) succeeded to the throne in 1407. During the long reign of John II, power was always held by people other than the king. The dual regency of Catherine of Lancaster and Ferdinand, duke of Peñafiel and brother of the late king, kept peace throughout the realm. Ferdinand, a forceful and capable statesman, prevented the nobility from making any gains. He also won important victories against the kingdom of Granada, the most important being that of Antequera (1410) from which he took the name Ferdinand of Antequera. After 1419, John II fell under the influence of Álvaro de Luna, a grandnephew of Pope Benedict XIII and a mysterious figure who freed the king from his bondage to the aristocratic oligarchy. Álvaro kept the king under his control. Exiled twice, he returned to the court, always with greater power, until a coalition

reign of Henry IV, it was valued at 2,000 and at 2,500 *maravedis*. All of these variations and increases in value did not come from variation in the metal; it was always composed of 8 ounces of silver with a small addition of copper, but the frequent debasement of *maravedis* and of other coins caused the value of silver money of the same weight to seem to be greater by comparison. Indeed, all the variations in the value of silver are taken, for the most part, from Antonio Nebrissensi's *Repetitionibus*.[20] In fact,

---

of the high nobility and John's second queen, Isabel of Portugal, led to his execution in 1453. The king died the following year.

The political and financial developments of Castile from the time of King Ferdinand the Holy to John II (ca. 1198–ca. 1454) can be summarized as follows: "Despite the political upheaval and dynastic wars, the foundations for a stable, strong, and centralized monarchy were laid down in this period. For instance, a comprehensive system of taxation was established. Most important among the taxes collected were the *servicio*, an extraordinary tax voted by the cortes during times of need that, by the fifteenth century, had become quite regular, and the *montazgo*, or *servicio y montazgo*, a tax on the transhumance. The *mesta*, in fact, became the main source of royal income after 1350. In addition, the *alcabala*, a sales tax, was turned into a permanent and generalized tax under Henry II and John I" (p. 138). (DMA, 3, 138, s.v. Castile)

20. Antonio de Nebrija (1441–1522), Spanish humanist, was born to an Hidalgo family at Lebrija, near Seville. Nebrija received his primary education at Lebrija, then went to the University of Salamanca in 1455. Five years later, he obtained a position at the Spanish College at the University of Bologna where he spent ten years studying theology and acquainting himself with Italian humanist scholarship. Like many other humanists, Nebrija wrote poetry, commented on classical literary works, and promoted the study of classical languages and literature. For a short time (1513–1515), he participated in the editing of the Complutensian Polyglot Bible at the invitation of Cardinal Francisco Jiménez de Cisneros, the archbishop of Toledo and primate of Spain. He is remembered primarily for introducing the critical philological scholarship of Italian humanism into Renaissance Spain. The title, *De Repetitionibus*, was commonly used for practical handbooks of jurisprudence (canon and civil law) at the time. (EtR, 4, 288–89, s.v. Nebrija, Antonio de)

the extant coins of these kings are all rough and are indications of the tendency to debase money during these years.

The Catholic rulers, Ferdinand and Isabella, stabilized this volatility by a law that set the price for 8 ounces of natural silver at 2,210 *maravedis*, but when minted at 2,278. This is the price, even today. Philip II diminished the quality and weight of the *maravedi*, but since it was by a slight amount, there was no change in the value of silver in relation to the *maravedis*. I think that the recent change in copper money will alter its value and make 8 ounces of silver the equivalent of more than 4,000 *maravedis*, as presently minted. Am I wrong?

7

ADVANTAGES DERIVED FROM ALTERATION OF COPPER MONEY

A careful examination and investigation of the advantages and disadvantages that result from altering copper money are in order so that the wise and prudent reader may consider calmly and without prejudice which issues are of greater weight and importance. This is the way to the truth that we seek.

First, when such a change is made, we are freed from an expenditure of silver. Lessening the quality of silver provides this advantage. For years, a great weight and many talents of silver used to be mixed with copper to no profit. Because the money weighs less, it is easier for the merchants to transport and use in trade (the cost of transport used to be high). The increased money supply expands commerce in the nation, while the desire of eager outsiders to get their greedy hands on gold and silver money is curtailed. Those who have it will share it willingly with others; thus, debts will be liquidated, farms will be cultivated in the hope of greater profit, and workshops (frequently idle for lack of money) will be busy. In short, there will be a greater abundance of flocks, fruit, and merchandise, of linen, wool, silk cloth, and of other commercial items. No doubt, abundance will produce affordable prices (whereas in the past only a few could find those who would lend them money for such goods—and then at great interest). In these circumstances, we will be content with our lot and plenty and have less need for outside merchandise. Importing goods diminishes our silver and gold and infects our people with foreign customs. Men born for war and arms are physically weakened by the softness of merchandise, and their warlike vigor of spirits is extinguished. Also, foreigners will not come to us as often as they used to, both because of our abundance of native merchandise and because of our money, which they will refuse to take back to their native land at no profit after it has been exchanged for their goods. In general, with the money received for their merchandise, they will purchase other items in our country, as convenient, and will transport them to their native land.

It is not insignificant that a good deal of money will flow into the king's treasury, for payment of his creditors to whom he has mortgaged his tax revenues—a major disaster—and this can be accomplished without injury to or complaint from anyone just by changing the value of money. The king will certainly profit greatly.

Thus, Pliny, in the passage cited above, confirms that the Romans by diminishing the weight of the *as* escaped from extreme straits and paid debts that weighed them down. The history of Alfonso XI, King of Castile (chap. 98), report the same phenomenon and those of Henry II for the fifth year (chap. 10)[1] report that he was relieved, after ridding himself by this means of most oppressive war debts. A great deal of money had been promised

---

1. The history of Henry II's reign was written by the Castilian Chancellor, Pedro López de Ayala (1332–1407), and is available in a modern critical edition under the title, *Crónica del rey don Pedro y del rey don Enrique, su hermano, hi jos del rey don Alfonso onceno*, 2 vols., ed. Germán Orduna, intro. Germán Orduna and José Luis Moure (Buenos Aires: SECRIT, 1994–1997).

to others but especially to Bertrando Klaquino[2] and to foreigners by whose aid he had stripped his brother of the kingdom.

The ancient Romans, and other nations in our time, used copper money exclusively with no admixture of silver or other precious metal. Indeed, this usage seems to have once been more usual and common with other monies because the Romans commonly called their money "copper." Perhaps this custom has influenced us to explain by *maravedis* the size of someone's property or yearly taxable income. The Spaniards once used gold *maravedis*, but, at a time when they had to make great changes, they removed all gold from the *maravedis*. Thus, we should not be astonished if silver is now removed from our money. It is of no use and never was of any advantage to anyone.

These advantages are important and should be considered. We will pass over the disadvantages that a diligent observer may claim to result from the recent intervention. Nothing in this life is entirely simple and free from all harm and blame. Therefore, it is the wise man's job to choose what affords the greater and less-blameworthy advantages, especially since human nature is perverse in such circumstances and is used to criticizing changes and new ways. We hold firmly to traditions, as if nothing could be corrected in, or added to the practices of the ancients.

---

2. Bertrand Du Guesclin (1314–1380), or Beltran Claquin, was the constable and protector of France, celebrated fourteenth-century mercenary, and the liberator of Spain. His colorful and intriguing life touched several notable figures in the period of mid to late fourteenth-century France. He had dealings with such prominent individuals as the duke of Lancaster, Charles de Blois, Charles V of France, Peter I of Castile and León, and Henry II of Castile and León, to mention only a few. See chapter 6, note 12, for more on his role in the assassination of Peter I. The *Bibliothèque historique de France* lists no less than nine manuscripts treating the life of Du Guesclin. (BU, 12, 169–80, s.v. DUGUESCLIN [Bertrand])

8

DIFFERENT *MARAVEDIS* OF VARYING VALUES IN CASTILE

Before I explain the disadvantages necessarily involved in the new plan for devaluing copper money, it is worth explaining the different kinds of *maravedis* and their values as used in Castile at various times. The understanding of these coins is involved and complicated but is worth having if we are to reach the truth that has been shrouded in darkness.

The gold coins in frequent use at the time of the Goths have first place. Indeed, the Romans in the later Empire struck coins of less weight than the old ones: They used to mint 6 coins from an ounce of gold, 48 from 8 ounces or a *mark*. These coins were a little bigger than our *castellano*. They called these gold coins *solidi*, and the value of each was 12 *denarii*. However, if the value of a Roman *denarius* was 40 *quadrantes* or *maravedis*, the value of a *solidus* came to 480—a little more than our *castellano*. Thus, in subsequent time, the *solidus*, although struck from silver and finally made for the greater part from copper, still always kept the value of 12 *denarii*—even when the latter were no longer made from gold but from copper. Certainly in France and among the people of Aragón, where the name *solidus* is still found, each *solidus* is worth 12 *denarii*. When the Goths invaded with the sword, the Roman Empire was still flourishing in Spain, as was Roman money, laws, and customs.[1] When government in Rome changed, the victors introduced some of their own customs and adopted some customs from the conquered. In particular, the Goths began to use Roman money. Then, when the new government was established, they devised and struck new coins that they called *maravedis*. There is no need to go into the meaning of the word, but each *maravedi* was valued at 10 *denarii*, or 400 *quadrantes*, as much as our current gold coin,[2] that is, 400

---

1. The Roman influence in law was an especially strong and enduring legacy. "The seventh-century Visigothic Code (*Leges Visigothorum*) contains a number of elements derived from Roman law. Roman law teaching was revived in non-Arabic Spain by the early thirteenth century, and by the middle of the century the various redactions of the *Fuero real* (between 1252 and 1255) and the *Libro de las leyes* (a later redaction of which is known as *Las siete partidas*) show a native legal system imbued with Roman ideas" (p. 422) (DMA, 7, 418–25, s.v. Law, Civil—*Corpus Iuris*, Revival and Spread).

More specifically, the Roman legal influence, which can be traced to the seventh century "work of four Visigothic kings, with the active participation of the church, through the famous councils of Toledo (the Eighth and Twelfth), led to the compilation of a highly romanized code, the *Liber iudiciorum* or *Lex barbara visigothorum* (not to be confused with the earlier *Lex romana visigothorum*, or Breviary of Alaric). Began probably under Chindaswinth (642–652), with the work continuing under his son Recceswinth (653–672), the *Liber iudiciorum* became the sole guide for the administration of justice in Visigothic Spain. All previous legislation ceased to have binding force in the king's court. The sources for the *Liber* were Leovigild's Code, Justinian's law codification ..., other assorted Roman legal texts, and St. Isidore's *Etymologies*.... The *Liber* consisted of twelve books. It included discussions of the law and the legislator, judicial organization and procedure, civil and criminal law, and a variety of other topics such as treatment of heretics, Jews, and the sick.... The *Liber iudiciorum* was undoubtedly the greatest legacy of Visigothic Spain. It far outlived the barbarian kings, influencing later Spanish legal systems and the law of the Spanish colonies around the world" (p. 520). (DMA, 7, 518–24, s.v. Law, Spanish)

2. The current gold coin during Mariana's time had the name *escudo*.

maravedis or *quadrantes*. It was established that the *maravedis*, although first made of silver and then of copper, would still be valued at 10 *denarii*.

The norm for the *maravedi* was that it would contain 2 *blancas*, 6 *coronados*, 10 *denarii*, 60 *meajas*. This was their relationship to the *maravedi*, although they completely disappeared because they were worthless. The Roman *solidus* and the Gothic gold *maravedi* differed little in value. Consequently, for the number of *solidi* imposed as punishment by the courts under Roman law, the Goths substituted a like number of gold *maravedis*. Many coins of the Goths are now being unearthed in Spain that are not made from good gold. We have evidence that their worth is debased by half: They are half-*maravedis*, coins called *semises* or rather, *tremisses*, weighing one-third of the Goths' *maravedi*.[3] We will consider this matter later.

---

3. Independent confirmation of Mariana's account of currency devaluation after the fall of Rome can be found in an essay by numismatic historian Mark Blackburn. According to Blackburn, "During the first two centuries following the collapse of the western empire, the currencies of the new barbarian kingdoms were based largely on locally produced gold coins. Only in Italy under Ostrogothic and later Byzantine control was a range of silver and bronze coins also issued in substantial quantity. The Franks, Burgundians, Suevi, Visigoths, Lombards, and Anglo-Saxons all had essentially mono-metallic currency systems based on the gold solidus and increasingly the tremissis (one-third solidus). However, apparent shortages of gold for currency in western Europe resulted in progressive reductions in fineness, seen first in the late sixth-century coinage of Visigothic Spain and during the early seventh century in that of the Franks. By the third quarter of the seventh century the fineness of the Frankish and Anglo-Saxon coins had fallen to as little as 25 percent gold or less alloyed with silver, and during the 670s these base gold tremisses were replaced by new coins of virtually pure silver. The old tremisses were quickly driven out of circulation leaving once again a mono-metallic currency in Francia and England" (p. 539).

"Elsewhere in Europe, in Italy and briefly in Spain, the use of gold coinages lingered on. The Visigothic tremisses of the late seventh century were heavily debased, but their issue continued until the Arab conquest of Spain in 711–15" (p. 540). See Mark Blackburn, "Money and Coinage," in

Tumultuous times followed. Everything, money included, was in a state of frightful confusion. After Spain was defeated by the weapons of the Moors,[4] a new race of kings sprang up, given by God for the salvation of a nation that was oppressed by every evil. We will not talk about the money of the Moors,[5] but there were three kinds of *maravedis* under the government of the kings of León and Castile.[6] There were the gold ones, which were also called *good, old, standard*, and *usual*. We must first speak about these *usual* ones and explain their value and quality because our understanding of the other types depends upon an explanation of the *usual* ones.

The value of the *usual* ones was not constant but changed with the times. It is difficult to define this variation: The only legitimate source for a guess is by reference to the value of a silver *mark*. These *maravedis* must be compared to our *maravedis* in

---

The New Cambridge Medieval History, vol. 2, *c. 700–c. 900*, ed. Rosamond McKitterick (Cambridge: Cambridge University Press, 1995), 538–59.

4. The Arab conquest of Spain took place from 711–715.

5. According to Blackburn, "The Umayyad governors replaced the Germanic system of coinage with an Arabic one, consisting initially of gold dinars and their fractions similar to those of North Africa but of inferior and very variable fineness. These coins belong to a transitional phase in which pseudo-Byzantine types were still giving way to purely Islamic ones in the western provinces of the caliphate. Between 711/712 and 720/721 (AH 93–102) three successive types of gold coinage were issued in Spain: Arab-Byzantine types with Latin inscriptions, Arab-Byzantine types with bilingual inscriptions, and Arabic types with entirely Kufic inscriptions. These Kufic dinars, of restored (*c.* 98 percent) fineness, were struck in small numbers down to 744/745 (AH 127), after which no further gold was issued in Spain for some two hundred years, until the Spanish Umayyads conquered North Africa, gaining access to Sudanese gold. The currency became one based essentially on silver dirhems weighing *c.* 2.9 g, more than twice as heavy as the Frankish denier, supplemented with some low-value copper coins." See Blackburn. "Money and Coinage," 540.

6. The united government of León and the primitive earldom of Castile, which had been ruled in common since 1035 under Ferdinand I, came to an abrupt end in 1230 with the reign of Ferdinand III (also known as Ferdinand the Holy).

the exact proportion as the *mark* of that age is compared to the value of the *mark* of our age. At this time, a bullion *mark* is worth 2,210 *maravedis*, but, once minted and made into coins—2,278 *maravedis*. Moreover, the quality of the silver does not enter into consideration: It has always been more or less of the same purity as today, as the chalices, and other sacred vessels and instruments, preserved in our Church treasuries, bear witness. Then the silver *mark*, in relation to the varying value of the *maravedi*, was always worth 5 gold coins (popularly called *doblas*)[7] or a little more, and equal to 12 silver coins—not 14, as some say. Likewise, the *mark* used to be worth 60 or 65 silver coins, as we can see from the laws of King John I of Castile, but debate rushes in from another source.

The oldest known value of the *mark* is 125 *maravedis*. This was certainly the value of the *mark* in the age of King Alfonso XI, as witnessed in the history of his accomplishments (chap. 98). Thus, a silver coin was just 2 *maravedis*; now it is 34. Therefore, a *maravedi* at that time was worth as much as 17 and a bit more of ours, and there was no doubt about the quality of the silver that its value declared. In the reign of Henry II, a silver coin was worth 3 *maravedis*, as the history of his fourth year (chap. 2) declares. Therefore, the *mark*, at this time, increased to 200 *maravedis*, each one equal to 11 of ours. Henry was succeeded by his son John I, and the *mark* increased under him to 250 *maravedis* or *quadrantes*, when a silver coin was valued at 4 *maravedis* and a gold one at 50 (see the first law he enacted in the parliament of the kingdom of Burgos in 1388). Thus, the *maravedi* of that time was equal in value to 9 or 10 of ours. Even more clear is a previous law promulgated in Burgos that punishes abuse of parents by a fine of 600 *maravedis*. During the reign of Ferdinand and Isabella, that law was introduced into the *Ordinamentum*[8] (bk.

---

7. Also known as *doubloons*.

8. The development of parliamentary institutions was a common phenomenon throughout western Europe from the thirteenth century on. In

8, title 9). It stated that the 600 *maravedis* mentioned in that law are good money and equal 6,000 *maravedis* in that time, which is also our own; for, since that time, there has been no change in the value of the *mark* or *maravedi*.

Let us look at the reigns of other kings. According to old documents, under Henry III the *mark* reached to 480 and even 500 *maravedis*. Therefore, a silver coin was worth about 8 *maravedis*, and the *maravedi* was equal to about 4 or 5 of ours. Under John II, Henry's son, the *mark* was worth 1,000 *maravedis*, especially at the end of his life. Thus, his *maravedi* was worth 2½ of ours—a remarkable variation in value! However, this fluctuation was not confined to his reign. Among many other serious ills, under Henry IV, the silver *mark* reached 2,000 *maravedis* and then 2,500, according to Antonio Nebrissensi's *Repetitionibus*. His *maravedi* was worth what ours is, and there has not been great change in the value of the *maravedi* since that time. This stability must be attributed to the care of Ferdinand and Isabella and their successors. With these facts established from laws and chronicles, let us evaluate the other *maravedis*.

Castile, León, Burgos, Aragón, Catalonia, and other provinces, the king traditionally consulted with the nobles and bishops of his curia on matters of significance. As towns became more important as centers of administration, trade, and industry, and as sources of military forces, their representatives were summoned to counsel the king. With that the *curia regis* was transformed into the *cortes*, which is the plural of *corte*, the Spanish vernacular term for the king's court. The cortes came to be viewed as an assembly of estates—prelates, nobles, and townsmen—who, together with the king, formed the body politic. The Castilian cortes submitted petitions to the crown that, on being drawn up as ordinances and approved by the king, had the full force of law. Alfonso XI in 1348 promulgated the *Ordenamiento de Alcalá*, an extensive law code prepared by his jurists, in the cortes. The principle that the laws enacted in the cortes could be abrogated only by the cortes was stated in 1305, 1313, 1379, and 1387. Of course, it goes without saying that new laws could always be added to the *Ordinamentum* as was the case with the law promulgated in Burgos concerning the abuse of parents. (DMA, 3, 610–12, s.v. Cortes)

The gold *maravedi* was equal to 6 of the *maravedis* current in the time of Alfonso the Wise. Law 114[9] of the *Lex stili*[10] states that after this king looked into the matter, he found that a gold *maravedi* was equal to 6 of the *maravedis* of his day. This is not, as some claim, that the *maravedis* of King Alfonso were made of gold. Rather, the value was discovered by weighing *maravedis* of both kinds, and from establishing their proportions of gold to silver—12 to 1. Moreover, the law of Alfonso XI in the parliament of León of 1387[11] stated that 100 *maravedis* of good money, namely, of gold, were worth 600 of those of that age. Two important things may be gathered from these facts. First, that from the time of King Alfonso the Wise (also known as the Tenth) up until Alfonso XI, his great-grandson, there was absolutely no change in the value of the *mark* and *maravedi*, inasmuch as under both kings the gold *maravedi* equaled 6 *usual* ones. Second, inasmuch as the *maravedis* then in use equaled 17 of ours (or even a little more, as mentioned above), those who said that the gold *maravedi* was equal to 36 or 60 of ours are necessarily mistaken. Rather, they were worth as much as 300 silver ones or more. This is my opinion, and it is founded on firm arguments. I am also of the opinion that the gold *maravedis* were the *tremisses* of the Goths. The first kings of Castile used them. They did not mint new ones. Their value agrees with the known one of a little more than 3 silver coins. These coins of the Goths turn up here and there, but no gold coins struck with the crest and name of the kings of Castile have been found at all. It

---

9. The Spanish text says, Law 144. Cf. Juan de Mariana, *Tratado y discurso sobre la moneda de vellón*, ed. L. Beltrán (Madrid: Instituto de Estudios Fiscales, 1987).

10. The 252 *Leyes del estilo* are laws pertaining to custom, the forms and arts of convention, for all types of formal proceedings. They date from the first half of the fourteenth century.

11. The text on this point is inaccurate. According to the record of the cortes, the parliament of León under Alfonso XI had enacted this policy already in the years 1342, 1345, and 1349.

would be incredible if all of them have disappeared without a trace. So much for the gold *maravedi*.

Most people say that each of the old *maravedis* was worth 1½ of ours. The pronouncements of those who have a greater understanding of our law will carry more weight on this issue. Perhaps there was agreement among the legal experts that, whenever the old *maravedi* occurs in our law, 1½ of ours may be substituted, just as the gold *maravedi* found in those laws is popularly evaluated at 36 or 60 of the *usual*.

However, strictly speaking, the old *maravedis* did not have one value but varying and complex values. Whenever the quality of money was diminished, as frequently happened to avoid abolishing the old money, the kings decreed that it should coexist with the new one and be called "old." Thus, it will be easy for some of the usual *maravedis* and those of the older kind to be compared with one another and with ours. If, for example, the *maravedi* of Alfonso XI is compared with the *maravedis* minted by his son, Henry II, it will be worth 1½ of the latter and, if compared with ours, it will be worth 17. Thus, the old *maravedis* were sometimes the usual *maravedis*. Therefore, from the value of the usual *maravedis*, as we have explained, one ought to establish the value of the old ones, and from those that are called "new," one ought to establish their value when compared with ours. These are subtle and thorny considerations, but we are hurrying to end this discussion. We add that, under our law, the *maravedis*, which are current today and were current in the time of the Catholic King Ferdinand, are commonly called "new." At this time, the laws of earlier kings were gathered together in a few volumes.[12] The *maravedis* of the earlier kings were called "old" *maravedis*.

Therefore, from the value of the *maravedi* in use under the individual kings, a decision may be made about the old *maravedi*. The *maravedi* of Alfonso XI was worth 17 of ours; that of

---

12. The new legal collection was given the title *Ordinamentum* (*Ordenanzas Reales de Montalvo*).

Henry II, 11; that of John I, 10; that of Henry III, 5; that of John II, 2½. Careful consideration must be given to the times, and determinations must be made accordingly concerning the value of an old *maravedi* in any law, and the value of a new one, both among themselves and in comparison with our own *maravedis*. It should not be overlooked that the old *maravedi* was sometimes called "good," as in the above-mentioned law (*Ordinamentum*, bk. 8, title 9) by which John I prescribed the punishment of 600 *maravedis* for the abuse of parents. The experts who incorporated this law in that book added on their own that the *maravedis* were good coins, equal to 6,000 of the *usual* ones. This means that the law was not referring to gold *maravedis* but to old ones that were in use under that king and that each was worth as much as 10 of ours. Remember that from the time of Ferdinand the Catholic the value of the *maravedi* remained unchanged.

Moreover, by a law passed by John II in Caraccas[13] in 1409 (the first law in *Ordinamentum*, bk. 8, title 5) something is forbidden under punishment of excommunication of thirty days and a fine of 100 good *maravedis*, which make 600 of the old ones. However, if the obstinacy continues for six months, the fine increases to 1,000 good *maravedis*, which equal 6,000 of the old ones. In this citation, the good *maravedis* are gold; the old ones are those that were current under the Kings Alfonso the Wise and Alfonso XI. Only at that time, as stated above, did each gold *maravedi* equal 6 current ones. If the punishment seems very harsh—it is equivalent to 3,000 of our silver ones, since each gold *maravedi* equals as much as 3 silver ones—even more serious punishments are inflicted today. When someone is suspected of heresy, he will not escape the bond of excommunication for a full year.

---

13. That is, the parliament of Guadalajara in 1409.

Finally, in the history of King John II[14] (the twenty-ninth year, chap. 144) a mandate was introduced in the parliament of Burgos for the minting of half-*maravedis*, which we call *blancas* because of their whiteness, in accordance with the quality and weight of the coinage of his father, Henry III. That money, however, was discovered to be inferior. When the affair was investigated and the defect and fault recognized, the procurators of the kingdom decreed that the previous *maravedi*, namely that of King Henry III, should be valued at 1½ of the new *maravedis*. This is related in this king's history (the forty-second year, chap. 36). By universal decree, from this time on, the procurators seem to have taken the opportunity to declare that an old *maravedi* was worth 1½ of ours, whereas they should have rather said that the *maravedi* minted by Henry III, was worth 1½ of those minted by John II. Indeed, if we consider the value of the *mark* under both kings, the defect was not adequately remedied, and the previous *maravedi* was worth fully 2 of the later ones. If a comparison is made with our *maravedi*, the *maravedi* of John II was worth 2½ of ours; the *maravedi* of Henry III was worth fully 4 or 5 of ours.

---

14. The history of John II's reign was originally thought to have been written by Álvar García de Santa María (1349–1460) but is now generally considered a compilation from the works of several authors, including the prominent Fernán Pérez de Guzmán (?1376–?1460). A modern critical edition of the *Crónica del serenissimo rey don Iuan*, ed. Angus Mackay and Dorothy Sherman Severin (Exeter: University of Exeter Press, 1981), is available with an English introduction and commentary that accompany the complete Spanish text.

9

DISADVANTAGES DERIVED FROM THIS ALTERATION OF COPPER MONEY

In serious issues, it is not fair to advance subtle and speculative arguments from our own heads and thoughts. They are frequently deceptive. It is better to do battle with data from our own time and from our ancestors. This is the safest approach and the assured way to the truth because the present is certainly similar to the past. What has happened will happen. Previous events are very influential: They convince us that what sets out on the same path will reach the same conclusion.

Some disadvantages appear to be great but, in reality, are not. We could put up with them to avoid the greater disadvantages that derive from the alteration of money. First, some critics claim that this practice has never been used in our country and that, because of its novelty, every innovation triggers fear and is risky. However, this argument is proved untrue by what has already been said. Obviously, this process has frequently been tried in our country. With what success is not yet the issue! They also argue that there has been less cultivation of the land and farms, and that citizens are discouraged from working when wages are paid in debased money. This is true. Among other advantages of alteration and multiplication of copper coins, however, is the fact that with this money on hand and available to everyone, the fruits of the earth and the products of handicraft will be more easily produced. In the past, they were frequently neglected for lack of money. Therefore, this argument proves inconclusive and because it can be used by either side, it is not convincing for either.

These critics then assert that commerce will be hindered, especially with those who come from outside Spain with the sole hope of exchanging their goods for our silver. Facts speak for themselves, they say, and debased coinage will create great havoc with commerce with the Indies because most things sent to that region are imported into Spain from outside nations. The answer to this objection is not difficult either. One may argue that it is no disadvantage for Spain to obey its own laws, as it is strictly forbidden to export silver to other nations. Moreover, how is it advantageous to despoil the country of its silver? Rather, it would seem beneficial if the copper money of commerce deterred outsiders from coming into Spain. Certainly, they will exchange their goods for our goods when the hope of carrying off our wealth has been removed. This is and should be the common desire of a nation. Further, there is no danger of harming trade with the Indies because it involves goods that are native to us: wine, oil, wool, and silk cloth. If there is need for commerce with outsiders, silver will arrive from the Indies now and then and allow our merchants to buy such things as linen cloth, paper, books, trifles, and so forth. Nor does copper money prevent us from minting this foreign silver, as we have done before. There is a ready response to the next objection that denies that the king has the authority to borrow money from outsiders to meet the necessary expenses of the fleet and the salaries of the soldiers. We might rather say that there would be a greater supply of money for the king if his debts to his countrymen were paid in copper money. He could pay his foreign debts in the silver that is offered to him every year. Nor is copper money so wicked or barren that silver will completely disappear, as if chased away by a wicked and magical incantation.

It is true, we must admit, that when there is a great supply of copper, silver disappears among the citizens. This fact should be numbered among the principal disadvantages of copper money. Silver flows into the royal treasury because the king orders that taxes are to be paid in that money. It does not return to circulation because he pays whatever he owes his subjects with copper money. Thus, there will be a superabundance of copper money while he exports the silver. Moreover, the silver that remains in our citizens' hands disappears because all first spend the copper money and hide the silver, unless forced to produce it.

Some argue that the great supply of debased money would bring about this disadvantage, but the reasons for their position are not satisfactory. They advance two reasons for their position: The first is that royal money cannot be distinguished from counterfeit money once the silver, which used to be mixed with the copper, has been completely removed; the second is that the hope of profit will tempt many. This profit is three times larger than before because, while the actual value of the money has changed little, the legal value has changed much. I will not dispute these arguments. How could I? The latter one, based on the hope of profit is quite valid, as 200 gold coins become 700 because of debased money. This fact will certainly tempt many to expose themselves and their possessions to any risk for profit. Who would bridle his inflamed desire suddenly to escape indigence in this way? However, the previous argument is not based on facts. It rests on the belief that silver was mixed with copper to prevent adulteration of copper money. In fact, the silver remains from the early quality of the *maravedi*, which was once solid silver but was later defiled with many additions. Nonetheless, some silver was always found in it. The first Catholic kings did not ordain this, but they determined by law how much silver was to be mixed with copper, lest the debasing of that money proceed further by an ever greater amount of copper. It would not be bad if no silver were mixed into copper money. As a matter of fact, the expense of silver would be avoided.

If my argument is in any way valid, I would like the stamp on coins to be more refined, as it is on coins from the mints in Segovia. Moreover, the silver *real* would be exchanged for more copper coins, as happens in France. There, 12 *dineros* are given for a silver *solidus*, which is almost a *cuartillo*,[1] and each *dinero* is worth 3 *liardi*. At Naples, a *carlino*, less than our silver coin, worth not more than 28 *maravedis*, is exchanged for 60 *caballi*, each with the weight and mass of 2 earlier *maravedis*, before they were constantly adulterated. All these facts confirm that the value of a silver coin is equal to the metal and the cost of minting, and this means accommodating the legal value to the natural value. Few people would undertake to debase that money because of less profit; nor would it be easy for ordinary people—and such, for the most part, are those who make counterfeit money—to maintain mints to coin similar money. If anyone does mold coins from melted copper, they will be readily distinguishable from struck money.

As a matter of fact, silver is minted in these mills at a great loss; coins of equal weight cannot be produced because of the variations in the silver ingots placed on the press. This disadvantage does not exist with copper because it is a base metal. I pass over the other proposed disadvantages—they are more apparent than true—to address greater disadvantages, which arise not from empty speculation but are proven by the experience of former times and the memory of antiquity. Critics add that with the multiplication of copper money and its currency, no fortunes would be piled up by the rich for use in pious works. Surely, so many people spend piles of money in harmful and ludicrous things that it would not seem to be a great loss if fortunes were not amassed. Copper money does not stand in the way of quanti-

---

1. That is, a quarter of a *real*.

ties of silver yearly arriving from the Indies. Who will prevent the owners from hoarding as much of the silver as they want? Others find fault with the cost of transportation: They do not wish the merchants to have to transport purchased goods from afar at that cost. However, those same merchants, after reckoning the cost of shipping to the end of the country (from Toledo to Murcia), claim that the expense is only 1 percent. Then, some say, it is very laborious to count this copper money and keeping it is particularly bothersome.

Others say that these troubles are sufficiently compensated for by the advantages that this money entails. Critics also find fault with the expense of copper because of the great amount minted, and they cite the difficulty of forging it at home. As a result, outsiders, who have a great deal of this metal, will grow rich at our expense. A few years ago, a hundred-weight of copper sold for 18 *francs* in France. Thus, 8 ounces (what we call the weight of a *mark*) was fixed at 13 *maravedis*; in Germany, it was even cheaper. Currently, the same weight is fixed, nonetheless, at 46 *maravedis* in Castile. Therefore, the price of minting copper money endlessly increases out of necessity or, rather, out of cupidity. This is a real, not fictitious disadvantage, but there are other much greater ones in comparison with which, this one—whatever damage it causes—could seem ridiculous and relatively unimportant.

10

MAJOR DISADVANTAGES
DERIVED FROM THIS
ALTERATION OF MONEY

First of all, the current large supply of copper money is against our Spanish laws. There is no limitation on gold and silver money in the 1497 decree of the Catholic kings.[1] An individual was allowed to mint as much of these metals as he had. They decreed, however, in the third law, that no more than ten million *maravedis* were to be struck, with the responsibility for this minting divided according to a determined ratio among seven mints. Then Philip II, king of Spain, decreed in a 1566 law that it was not advantageous to manufacture more copper money than would be enough for common use and commerce. He therefore commanded that such money was not to be minted without royal authorization.

Moreover, copper money should be commonly employed only in small purchases, and gold or silver was to be used in greater monetary exchanges. Anything beyond these limits would involve public damage and upheaval, for money was invented to

---

1. This is a reference to the monetary policy promulgated by King Ferdinand and Isabella in Medina del Campo in 1497.

facilitate trade, and money that better and more opportunely accomplishes its end is more acceptable, as Aristotle remarks in his *Politics* (bk. 1, chap. 6).[2] However, abundance of copper money brings about the opposite. Counting it is a great burden: A man can hardly count a thousand gold pieces in copper coins in a day. As for transporting coins, it is laborious and expensive to carry them to distant places to buy goods. For these reasons, an inundation of this money is opposed by our laws. Of course, I would not approve of minting just silver money as, for example, in England under the recently deceased Queen Elizabeth[3] and in some German states. I realize that it can be divided into tiny parts. It is said that Renato,[4] the Duke of Anjou, made a thou-

---

2. Mariana's reference to chapter 6 of book 1 is inaccurate. Aristotle addresses the creation of currencies to facilitate exchange over vast distances (the portability of money idea) and to serve as a measure in exchanges in book 1, chapter 9 of the *Politics*.

3. Elizabeth I (1533–1603), reigned as Queen of England's golden age from 1558 to her death, and was the architect of England's final break with the papacy. She was the daughter of Henry VIII and Anne Boleyn, whom Henry accused of adultery and executed. Even with this frightful beginning, Elizabeth enjoyed a peaceful childhood and was educated in the new learning by such brilliant English humanists as Roger Ascham. The long reign of Elizabeth I was one of the most remarkable in English history, and the Queen was a legend in her own lifetime. During these forty-five years, English Protestantism and English nationalism achieved success, and England experienced new maritime supremacy, a strengthened economy, and a brilliant literary vitality. (NCE, 5, 281–82, s.v. Elizabeth I, Queen of England)

4. René I (1409–1480), duke of Anjou, count of Provence and of Piedmont, king of Naples, Sicily, and Jerusalem was the second son of Louis II, king of Sicily, duke of Anjou, count of Provence, and of Yolande of Aragón. Louis II died in 1417, and his sons, together with their brother-in-law, afterwards Charles VII of France, were raised under the guardianship of their mother. The elder, Louis III, succeeded to the crown of Sicily and to the duchy of Anjou, René being known as the count of Guise. When his brother Louis III and Jeanne [Giovanna] II de Duras, queen of Naples, died, René succeeded to the kingdom of Naples. Louis had been adopted

sand coins out of an ounce of silver (I would prefer a pound). With these coins, however, one could not buy tiny and cheap trinkets and give alms to the needy. Much greater harms result if the abuse is in the other direction—if the land is inundated with copper money like rivers flooded with winter storms. So much for the first disadvantage.

A second disadvantage is not only that it is against the laws of the land—that could be overlooked—but it is also against right reason and the natural law itself—it is a sin to change them. To prove my point, one must remember what was established above: The king is not free to seize his subjects' goods and thus strip them from their lawful owners. May a prince break into granaries and take half of the grain stored there, and then compensate for the damage by authorizing the owners to sell the remainder at the same price as the original whole? No one would be so perverse as to condone such an act but such was the case with the old copper coin. The king unjustly appropriated one-half of all the money, merely by doubling the value of each coin, so that what was worth 2 *maravedis* was thereafter worth 4. Would it be right for a king to triple by law the price for woolen and silk cloth at its present supply, while the proprietor keeps one-third for himself and turns over the rest only to the king? Who would approve of that? The same thing is happening with the copper

---

by Jeanne II in 1431, and she left her inheritance to René. The marriage of Marie de Bourbon, niece of Philip of Burgundy, with John, duke of Calabria, René's eldest son, cemented peace between the warring Burgundian princes of Philip the Good and Antoine de Vaudemont. In 1438, René set sail for Naples, which had been held for him by the Duchess Isabel. His prior captivity and ransome enabled Alfonso V of Aragón, who had been first adopted and then repudiated by Jeanne II, to make some headway in the kingdom of Naples as he was already in possession of the island of Sicily. In 1441, Alfonso laid siege to Naples, which he sacked after six months. René returned to France the same year, and though he retained the title of king of Naples he never recovered his rule. (EB, 23, 97–98, s.v. René I)

money that has recently been minted. Less than a third of it is given to the owner. The king uses the rest for his own advantage.

Such things, of course, do not take place in other forms of commerce. They do, however, happen in the arena of money because the king has more power over money than over other things. He appoints all the ministers of the mint and changes them at will; he controls the dies and types of money, has complete authority to change them and to substitute debased coins for purer ones, and vice versa. Whether this is done rightly or wrongly is a controversial point. However, Menochius[5] (*Consilium*, no. 48) deems it a new kind of crime to repay, with debased money, debts incurred at a time when money was sound. He proves with many arguments that what was paid out in sound money is not rightly repaid in debased money.

We come to the third disadvantage: The cost of trade will be in proportion to the debasing of money. This is not simply a private judgment. Rather, such were the evils our ancestors experienced when our money was debased. In the history of the reign of Alfonso the Wise (chap. 1), reference is made to alteration of money at the beginning of his reign: Less sound *burgaleses* were substituted for the usual sound money, *pepiones* (gold coins). Ninety copper *burgaleses* were equal in value to a *maravedi*. This money change resulted in a general inflation. To remedy this situation, as chapter 5 recalls, the king taxed all sales. His remedy, however, caused the ailment to break out again. The merchants refused to sell things at that price. Necessarily, things came to a halt lest he arouse the hatred of the nation or especially (as we believe) the arms of his nobles, who, after he was driven out, transferred affairs to his younger son, Sancho. Not content with his previous fraudulent mistake, he substi-

---

5. Giacomo Menochio (1532–1607) was a famous legal scholar and professor of law at Pavia (1556–1560, 1588–1607), Mondovi (1561–1566), and Padova (1566–1588). Mariana cites his main work, *Consiliorum sive responsorum liber quartus* (Venice: Franciscum Zilettum, 1584).

tuted the recalled *burgaleses* with bad money with the value of 15 *maravedis* in the sixth year of his reign. Thus, he remained obstinate in evil—a man deceitful by nature with a shattered genius that was ultimately evil.

The history of King Alfonso XI of Castile (chap. 98) informs us that he minted *novenes* and *coronados* of the same quality and stamp as his father, King Ferdinand. To avoid inflation with the change of money—doubtless it was not sound—great care was taken to keep the price of silver from rising. Eight ounces of silver were valued at 125 *maravedis*—no more than before. This concern was feckless. There ensued scarcity of goods, and the price of silver increased. Here we should consider the fact that inflation is not the immediate and necessary consequence of changing money. As a matter of fact, a silver coin is now worth 34 of these debased *maravedis*—its previous worth—and 8 ounces of silver (which we call a *mark*) sells for 65 silver coins as it actually did before. Our account has made it clear that this condition cannot continue longer without disturbance. John I, in order to pay his rival, the Duke of Alencastre, a great sum of money, which had been agreed upon, minted unsound money, which he called "good." Shortly thereafter to avoid a scarcity of goods, he approved its payment at almost less than half, as he testified in the 1387 parliament of Burgos.

Then, there is Henry II, the father of John. As head of the kingdom, he had almost exhausted his treasury in wars against his brother Peter. Finally, reduced to dire financial straits, he minted two kinds of money: *regales*, worth 3 *maravedis*, and *cruzados*, worth 1 *maravedi*. As a result, prices and other things increased. The gold coin, known as the *dobla*, rose to 300 *maravedis*; a *caballo* was selling at 60,000 *maravedis*. This fact is found in his chronicles (the fourth year, chap. 10). Indeed in the sixth year, chapter 8, the *caballo* rose to 80,000 *maravedis*. Inflation soared. Under this pressure, this prince decreed devaluation of each coin by two-thirds. Indeed the gold coin was previously worth 30 *maravedis*, as Antonio Nebrissensis states in his *Repetitionibus* and as may be deduced from the value of silver, of which, 8 ounces, or a *mark*, were valued at 125 *maravedis* or certainly a little less (see chapter 8 of this treatise for an explanation of gold and silver's increase in value at that time). As a result of the alteration in coinage, the value of gold suddenly increased almost more than tenfold. I am convinced that there is never an alteration in coinage without subsequent inflation. To illustrate, let us suppose that the value of silver is doubled: What was worth 34 *maravedis* is now worth 68.

Some believe and maintain that if the value of silver were increased, the state would benefit to a greater or lesser degree. If this is true, one must ask: If someone wishes to buy 8 ounces of debased silver for 65 silver coins as its value is set by law, would the seller comply? Of course not! He will not sell it for less than 130 new silver coins, which is almost the weight of the silver itself. However, if the value of silver is doubled because the value of coins is doubled or if the coins increase to sixfold or fourfold, the same thing will happen with the value of natural silver. We see the same thing happen with the current copper coins; they are changed in some places into silver coins at the rate of 100 percent interest; in other places at 50 percent. Doubtless, what we have shown to occur in the case of silver will happen to other commodities as well: Their price will increase to the degree that the coins have been debased or the value of the coins increased, for that is exactly the way it is.

There is no doubt that it leads to new money. Each of these developments will contribute to commercial inflation. Abundance of money makes it worth less. As in other commercial enterprises, supply leads to low prices. Next, the baseness of coins will cause those who have this money to want to get rid of it immediately. Merchants will not wish to exchange their goods for that money, except with a great increase in price. All this leads to the fourth disadvantage: There will be trade difficulties, and trade is the foundation for public and private wealth. This problem always arises with debasement of money. Taxation of goods and sales to increase prices is a rather deadly solution to the problem. This approach is burdensome for merchants, and they will refuse to sell at that price. Once trade is destroyed and commercial inflation is in place, all the people will be reduced to want, and that will lead to disturbances. Thus, as experience has frequently taught us, the new money is either completely recalled or is certainly devalued; for example, by half or two-thirds. Then, suddenly and as in a dream, someone who had 300 gold pieces in this money, now has 100 or 150, and the same proportion applies to everything else.

King Henry II, according to his chronicles (sixth year, chap. 8), faced this situation and of necessity devalued the *real* from its previous worth of 3 *maravedis* to 1 and reduced the *cruzado* to 2 *coronados*, a third of its previous value. Henry's son, John I, devalued his good money to 6 *dineros*, almost half of its previous value. The resulting inflation continued, as the king admits in the 1388 parliament at Burgos. There is no need to recount how much trouble occurred in the regions. The facts speak for themselves. At the end of chapter 8, we noted occurrences of this type under John II. Eduardius Nunnius[6] recalls in his *Chronicles of Portugal* that, under King Ferdinand,[7] a great inflation resulted

---

6. Duarte Nunez do Lião (1528–1608) was the resident scholar at the court of Sebastian of Portugal (1554–1578). His intellectual pursuits encompassed such diverse areas as economics, law, and national history, and his published works, which were largely written in Portuguese, treated these subjects in considerable detail. Mariana's reference is to his *Primeira parte das chronicas dos reis de Portugal*, 2 vols. (Lisbon: M. Coelho Amado, 1774). This work was originally published in Lisbon around 1600.

7. Ferdinand I of Portugal (1345–1383) succeeded to the throne in 1367. The wealthiest by far of the Portuguese monarchs to that time, Ferdinand did much to promote commerce and shipbuilding, and his economic legislation has justly been praised. The positive achievements during Ferdinand's reign have been obscured, however, by his three costly and disasterous wars with Castile and by his marriage to the controversial Leonor Teles, who was already married to someone else at the time of her marriage to Ferdinand. (DMA, 10, 52, s.v. Portugal: 1279–1481)

in Portugal because of the devaluing of money and that a large amount of this counterfeit money was brought in by foreigners. He also says that the younger people, of necessity, viewed this money with a singular severity because many people were reduced to helplessness. Nonetheless, he says that, in our time, the same error was imprudently committed. During the reign of Sebastian,[8] they minted copper money, called *batacones*, with the same evil results and the need to institute the same remedies.

Let us pass over the old examples, although what happened in Portugal is not that old. Sanderus[9] in his first book, *De schis-*

---

8. Sebastian of Portugal (1554–1578) succeeded to the throne in 1557 following the death of Dom João III. Sebastian, a young child and grandson to Dom João III, now embodied all the hopes of the Avis dynasty. However, Sebastian was chronically ill, both physically and mentally. Although he lived into adulthood, his weakness and unwillingness to leave an heir left considerable doubts about the dynasty's future. These doubts were realized in 1578 when Sebastian was killed in the battle of Alcacer Kebir (Qsar al-kabir) in an ill-conceived attempt to rekindle the Portuguese conquest in Morocco. His elderly great-uncle, Cardinal Dom Henrique, a caretaker king, proved unable to manage a smooth dynastic transition. A brief war of succession ensued in 1580, but Philip II of Spain met little resistance in laying claim to the throne of Portugal, which temporarily united Spain and Portugal. (EtR, 5, 135, s.v. Portugal)

9. Nicholas Sanders (1530–1581) was a controversial English historian and covert agent of the Roman Catholic Church during the reign of Queen Elizabeth I. He left England shortly after Elizabeth's accession to the throne and went to Rome where he obtained the doctor of divinity degree. He was present at various sessions of the Council of Trent and was a member of the theological faculty at the University of Louvain from 1565 to 1572. During his later years, he tried to stimulate resistance to Elizabeth's government and was commissioned by the papacy to go to Ireland for the purpose of inciting the Irish chieftans to rebellion. The work of Sanders that Mariana references—*De origine ac progressu schismatis Anglicani libri tres: quibus historia continetur maximè ecclesiastica, annorum circiter sexaginta … ab anno 21. regni Henrici octaui … usque ad hunc vigesimum octauum Elisabethae …* (Ingolstadt: Wolfgangi Ederi, 1587)—remained incomplete at his death. Despite its unfinished state, however, the book became a repository

mate Anglicano, affirms that, as he left the Church, Henry VIII[10] rushed into evils, and one of them was the fact that there was such a great devaluation of money. Consequently, whereas previously only a one-eleventh part of copper was mixed with silver coins, he gradually caused the coins to have no more one-sixth part silver to five parts copper. Then he ordered the old coins gathered into the treasury, and exchanged with an equal number of the new coins. A great injustice! After his death, the citizens approached his son Edward[11] for a cure for these evils. The

---

of source material for many Roman Catholic accounts of the English Reformation. (NCE, 12, 1048–49, s.v. Sander, Nicholas [Sanders])

10. Henry VIII (1491–1547) succeeded to the throne in 1509. Known principally for his break with Rome over the divorce of his first wife, Catherine of Aragón, Henry has been described as "a man with grandiose plans, but without the energy and, perhaps, the skill to execute them.... Henry was no working monarch; for two long stretches of his reign (c. 1513–1529 and *c.* 1532–1540), first Cardinal Thomas Wolsey and then Thomas Cromwell held sway, and royal government was virtually shed by the King and placed upon the chief minister." Throughout his career, Henry was hungry for glory and titles and viewed himself as a warrior king, which resulted in several skirmishes with France and Scotland, particularly during his latter years. Henry's wars with France and Scotland were costly and necessitated several debasements of the coinage to increase the royal treasury. Tragically, he was so preoccupied with Europe and his own domestic affairs that he showed no interest in the lucrative possibilities of the New World. "As a result, when England at last entered this field later in the century, it found itself generations behind the Spanish and Portuguese. But above all Henry had failed to turn to good use the vast new powers and the wealth that the Reformation had brought him." (NCE, 6, 1025–1029, s.v. Henry VIII, King of England)

11. Edward VI of England (1537–1553) succeeded to the thrones of England and Ireland in 1547. Edward was born at Hampton Court Palace to Henry VIII and Jane Seymour, Henry's third wife. His reign, though brief, was auspicious, as it marked the official beginning of England's Protestant Reformation. Edward himself, however, played no part in making royal policy. The authority to govern during his minor years lay with the sixteen executors of Henry VIII's will, the members of Edward's privy council. Edward Seymour, duke of Somerset, assumed power in March

only solution was to devalue the new money by half. Elizabeth, Edward's sister, succeeded him, and devalued the new money by another half. Thus, someone who had 400 coins in that money quickly found them reduced to no more than 100. Therefore, the cheating continued. When the problems connected with this money did not slacken, a new decree had all that money remitted to the mints in the hope of compensation. Such compensation was never made. An infamous highway robbery! A most disgraceful peculation!

A prudent reader should notice whether we are getting on the same road; whether that historical moment is a portrait of the tragedy certainly threatening us. The fifth disadvantage, the king's subsequent poverty, may not be greater than the ones already mentioned, but it is certainly inevitable. A king receives no income from his ruined subjects and cannot prosper when the country is sick. Both these reasons are closely connected. If the citizens are crushed with penury and if trade is in turmoil, then who will pay the king his customary revenue? The tax collectors will collect much less royal tribute. Are these statements dreams? Are they not verified by much history?

When Alfonso XI, king of Castile, was still a minor, his guardians were forced to render an account for all the royal revenues. It was discovered that all together they did not exceed 1,600,000 *maravedis*, as found in his history (chap. 14). Those *maravedis*

1547 as lord protector of the realm and governor of the king's person. A zealous Protestant, he abolished the Mass and other "idolatries" and invaded Scotland in 1547. Consequently, war with Scotland brought war with France, which nearly bankrupted England. When rebellious peasants challenged his authority in 1549, a group of councilors led by John Dudley, earl of Warwick, abolished the protectorate in a bloodless coup. Dudley (the duke of Northumberland after October 1551) ruled from 1550 on. He made peace with France and restored royal finance. He respected Edward VI's desire for religious reform, thus giving Thomas Cranmer, archbishop of Canterbury, freedom to reform further the doctrines and liturgy of the Church of England and to develop the Book of Common Prayer. (EtR, 2, 254–56, s.v. Edward VI)

were, of course, worth more than ours: Each one was worth 17 of our current ones. Nevertheless, it was a remarkably paltry income and seemed incredible. The historian ascribes two reasons for so great a disaster: the first, the greediness of the nobles who possessed many towns and strongholds of the kingdom; the other that, from the time of Ferdinand, five kings had altered money either by debasing it or increasing its value. In this way, with trade hampered and the nation reduced to penury, the nation's common disadvantage reached the king.

We conclude with the final disadvantage, the greatest of them all: The general hatred that will be stirred up for the prince. As a certain historian says, everyone takes responsibility for prosperity, the head is responsible for adversity.[12] How was the victory lost? Obviously, the supreme commander was imprudent in organizing his battle lines, or he did not pay the soldiers the salary

---

12. Mariana is likely making reference here to a passage by the Latin historian P. Cornelius Tacitus (c. 56–? AD) in his *Life of Agricola*, the biography of his father-in-law Gnaus Julius Agricola (40–93 AD), Roman governor of Britain for seven years from 77 (or 78) to 84 (or 85). After prevailing in a surprise night attack by the British, as Tacitus recounts, Agricola's Roman army "grew fierce and bold, presuming nothing could resist their Courage: They cried out, to be led into *Caledonia*, that by a continued Series of Victories, they might be brought to the utmost Limits of *Britain*" (p. 25). Tacitus observes, however, "the *Romans* returned, not fighting for Safety, but Glory and Honour" (p. 24). Yet, due largely to Roman vainglory and arrogance, the counterattack resulted in a bloody stalemate. "This is the unjust Condition of War, that all claim their Share in good Success, but bad is imputed but to one: The *Britains* supposing themselves defeated, not by the Courage of their Adversaries, but Conduct of their General, who had watched his Opportunity, abated nothing of their Arrogance, but lifted the stoutest Men they had, and carried their Wives and Children to Places of the greatest Security. The Cities confederated together, meeting frequently, and by Religious Rites, and offering up Sacrifices, confirmed their Association: And thus both Armies parted with equal Animosity" (p. 25). See *The Life of Agricola*, trans. John Potenger, in *The Annals and History of Cornelius Tacitus: His Account of the Antient Germans and the Life of Agricola*, vol. 1 (London: Matthew Gillyflower, 1698).

owed them. About 1300 AD, Philip[13] the Fair, king of France, was the first-known French king to debase money. As a result, Dante,[14] a celebrated poet of the time, called him "a forger of money." Robertus Gaguinus[15] reports in his life of the king that Philip, at his death, repented his deed and told his son, Louis

---

13. Philip IV of France (1268–1314), called the Fair, succeeded to the throne in 1285. After his father's death in the abortive Crusade against Aragón, a young Philip was forced to cope with a hopeless war and a heavy debt. Moreover, as the heir of crusaders, the grandson of a saint, and the ruler of the largest Roman Catholic country in Europe, Philip thought the French monarch was as necessary for human welfare as the Roman See. In an effort assert his sovereignty over territories he felt belonged to France, Philip engaged in costly warfare with England and Flanders. "These wars, fought with paid soldiers, were very expensive. Philip was always short of money; his greatest innovations and his greatest mistakes were due to the fact that he was near bankruptcy during most of his reign. He imposed the first general taxes in French history; he inflated currency; he expelled the Jews and confiscated their property; he abused judicial procedures to extort large fines from clergy, barons, and towns." (NCE, 11, 271–72, s.v. Philip IV, King of France)

14. Dante Alighieri (1265–1321), called "The Poet," is considered to be the father of Italian literature. He is reputed to have been the most learned layman of his time and deeply versed in theology. His *Divine Comedy* places Dante in the highest eschalon of literary accomplishment in the western canon. His *De monarchia libri tres*, though lesser known, presented an understanding of the "universal" monarch's sovereignty that epitomized political relations in the high Middles Ages. Dante made several critical jibes in relation to Philip IV, as seen from a casual perusal of the indexes to his major works. (DMA, 4, 94–105, s.v. Dante Alighieri)

15. Robert Gaguin (1433–1501), humanist rhetorician and general of the Maturin order, was employed as a diplomat/envoy in the service of several kings, including Louis XI, Frederick III, Charles VIII, and Louis XII. He wrote several multivolume histories during his lifetime. Mariana is likely referring to his *Compendium suprà Francorum gestis à Pharamundo usque ad annum* (Paris: André Brocard, 1491). (BU, 16, 265–69, s.v. GAGUIN [Robert])

Hutin,[16] that he had to put up with his people's hatred because he had debased the coinage and that Louis Hutin, therefore, was to correct his father's mistakes and hearken back to old reckonings. This concern proved useless. Before the people's hatred was defused, the one responsible for the monetary disaster, Enguerrano Marinio,[17] was publicly freed at the command of King Hutin, with the encouragement of some nobles and the approval of the whole land. This was a clear-cut crime, but it did not prevent the future kings from following in the same footsteps. French history

---

16. Louis X of France (1289–1316) succeeded to the throne in 1314. In 1314, leagues of nobles and towns were in rebellion against Philip IV's unpopular taxes for an abortive military campaign in Flanders, and the king's daughters-in-law had recently been involved in an adultery scandal. Louis attempted to defuse the political opposition, "mainly by issuing charters of reform to various regions. Historians have considered it significant that the French rebels (mostly nobles) did not demand or receive a national Magna Carta but were content with specific charters addressed to the particular interests of their localities. Regional particularism remained a potent factor in France, placing limitations on the scope of opposition to the crown but also preventing the crown from establishing common, centralized policies or institutions. Despite the expansion of royal power and institutions of government in the preceding reigns, France lacked a sense of 'community of the realm.' Like his father, Louis X needed money to fight the Flemings and experimented with representative assemblies. Louis did not use the latter merely for propaganda but tried to have them endorse royal taxes. His early death cut short this effort." (DMA, 5, 181, s.v. France: 1314–1494)

17. Enguerrand de Marigny (1260–1315) was Philip IV's prime minister. After becoming royal chamberlain in 1304, Marigny increasingly gained the king's confidence. By 1311, he was an important figure and by 1313–1314, the most influential adviser of the King. "He was prudent and skillful both as a diplomat and financial expert; he avoided unnecessary expenses and preferred negotiation to war. He helped to settle the difficulties arising out of the attack on Boniface VIII and tried to end the war with Flanders through a reasonable peace treaty." Charles of Valois, however, disliked Marigny's prudence and resented his influence. Thus, when Philip died, Charles brought false charges against Marigny, and succeeded in having him condemned to death. (NCE, 9, 221, s.v. Marigny, Enguerrand de; DMA, 5, 181–82, s.v. France: 1314–1494)

makes clear that Charles the Fair,[18] the brother of Hutin, caused a lot of trouble for his people. There is a law extant against him, the *De crimine falsi* of John XXII,[19] the Supreme Pontiff, and of Philip of Valois,[20] cousin and successor to both of these kings.

18. Charles IV of France (1294–1328), called the Fair, succeeded to the throne in 1322 and immediately faced problems over the uncertainty of succession, a need to devise a systematic form of taxation, and the requirement of living up to the traditional moral demands of French kingship. "Charles IV was particularly astute in making do with revenues of an extraordinary nature (seizures of the chattels of the returned Jews and of the profits of Italian bankers, for example). He was also successful in restoring a good deal of the moral image of the monarchy. Even in war—in Guienne and Flanders—he enjoyed temporary military successes without exciting, by his modest taxation, the rebellious opposition of his subjects. During peaceful interludes he refrained from exacting subsidies, obedient to the principle that when the cause of the subsidy ceases, the subsidy itself must cease. Below the surface, of course, historians can see unresolved major problems; but to the educated or influential Frenchman of 1328, the year of Charles' death, the monarchy strengthened by Philip Augustus, hallowed by Louis IX, and made conscious of its destiny by Philip the Fair, seemed to have weathered the stormiest period in a century with little loss of prestige." (DMA, 5, 172–73, s.v. France: 1223–1328)

19. This law concerns the crime of fraud.

20. Philip VI of France (1293–1350) succeeded to the throne in 1328. Early in 1328, Charles IV sickened and died, thereby opening the second phase of the royal succession crisis. Charles had no sons, and even before he died, the nobles decided that his first cousin, Philip of Valois, would be regent, becoming king if the pregnant queen did not bear a son. The problem with this arrangement was that Philip had no claim to Champagne or Navarre, strategic lands that were rich in latent revenue. Champagne and Navarre were supposed to pass to Joan, Louis X's daughter, who was married to her cousin, Philip of Évreux. Philip and the Valois managed these lands so poorly that Joan and the Évreux family held a grudge. A second problem for Philip concerned Edward III of England, Charles IV's nephew and the nearest male relative of Charles IV. At the time of Charles' death, Edward was ruled by his unpopular mother and he now headed the Plantagenet family, France's ancient enemy. The nobles were concerned, in Edward's case especially but even more generally, to reserve the throne of France to the male line and thus eliminate future conflicting claims.

Because of well-remembered misfortunes, the people of Aragón, in their dedication to, and interest in holding onto their freedom, demand from the king at his coronation an oath that he will never alter money. Petrus Belluga[21] mentions this point when he presents the two privileges granted to the people of Valencia by their kings in 1265 and 1336 (*Speculo Principum*, rubric 36, no. 5).[22] This is, doubtless, a healthy and prudent precaution.

Philip began his reign with a military victory over Flemish rebels in 1328, but relations with England steadily deteriorated in the 1330s. Philip was unsuccessful in pushing the people to abandon their historic hostility to taxation, an attitude that made collection of significant taxes impossible until outright fighting was in progress. This led many to think that the war with England was not a threat to their vital interests. However, after a series of defeats in 1340s, the Estates General of late 1347 authorized an extremely large tax to finance an effective army. As this was occurring, the Black Plague arrived in Europe and disrupted everything. (DMA, 5, 183–84, s.v. France: 1314–1494)

21. Peter Belluga (?–1468) was born in Valencia and worked as a jurist and counsellor to Alfonso V of Aragón (1416–1458). Alfonso V's costly efforts to maintain his family's interests in Castile were unpopular in the Crown of Aragón. From 1420 to 1423, he increased his power in the Mediterranean (Sardinia, Sicily, and Corsica). "In Naples he secured Queen Giovanna's recognition as her heir, then lost that fragile prospect to Louis III of Anjou, whose brother René finally succeeded her in 1435. After a time in Spain (1423–1432) Alfonso returned to Sicily, and through tortuous negotiation and fighting conquered Naples (1436–1443)." The original title of Belluga's work is *Speculum principum ac iustitiae* (Paris, 1530). (DMA, 1, 417, s.v. Aragón, Crown of (1137–1479)

22. The special privileges of the people of Valencia had been fixed by the order and deposition of the kings through a general charter, the "Council of One Hundred," dating back to 1265. The 1265 charter was part of a larger move to institute the cortes system in Valencia as was the case already in Aragón and Catalonia. "In local government royal judges supplemented the vicars, who remained officers of justice, police, and muster in Catalonia. James I actively promoted urban life. A series of charters to Barcelona (1249–1274) attributed increasing administrative autonomy to the elected counselors and the assembly; the 'Council of One Hundred' dates from 1265. The commerical law of Barcelona was codified in the *Libre del*

Greed causes blindness; financial straits create pressure; we forget the past. In this way, the cycle of evils returns. Personally, I wonder if those in charge of affairs are ignorant of these things. If they do know them, I wonder why they so rashly, despite their prudent knowledge, wish to rush headlong into these perils.

---

consolat del mar (Book of the Sea Consulate) one of a remarkable series of legal compilations in the mid-thirteenth century that include the customs of Valencia, Aragón, and Lérida, and the *Commemorations* of Pere Albert." (DMA, 1, 413, s.v. Aragón, Crown of [1137–1479])

11

SHOULD SILVER MONEY BE ALTERED?

All the disadvantages that we have explained as coming from adulteration of copper money are found more forcefully in the case of silver money because of its quality and abundance. Gold money is always less used, and if the government is prudently administered, there will not be a great supply of copper money. Actually, silver is the backbone of commerce because it is conveniently exchanged for all other goods and used to liquidate contracted debts. Some, however, are not affected by the disadvantages derived from the debasing of copper coinage. They maintain that debasing silver coins would greatly benefit the state. I have therefore decided to explain now whether such a move would correct the damage experienced or cause all affairs of state to be subverted, everything going topsy-turvy. I personally believe that the latter will happen. Would that I were a false prophet!

This approach, they say, is the way to safety and peace. Outsiders will not be enticed by its quality to lay their greedy hands on our silver and seek profit by diverting it to other nations. Meanwhile, our legal provisions are rendered powerless through fraud and ambition. It is a fact that Spanish silver money is better than that of its neighbors by at least a one-eighth part. Although they do not go into it, silver would be a greater means of curing the king's financial needs, for, if from the exchange of base copper money of little value they bring into the treasury over 600,000 gold pieces, can we imagine what would happen if silver were debased? It is in great supply in Spain, and each year—incredibly—a greater amount is imported from the Indies. There is the further advantage—that we have no need to get this metal from outsiders, as we do, at great expense, with copper. When they exchange their copper for our silver and gold, they gain a greater benefit—one is reminded of Glaucus and Diomedes.[1]

Certainly, we could make a huge profit if the silver were debased by a third or a fourth. Consider, for example, that silver could be devalued in three different ways. First, its value can be increased while the coin remains intact. Then, a silver coin, now worth 34 *maravedis*, would by law increase to 40, 50, or 60. Second, the weight could be diminished. We currently strike 67 silver pieces from 8 ounces of silver. In this situation, we would strike 80 or even 100, and each coin would continue to have its earlier value of 34 *maravedis*. On examination, this approach differs little from the previous one because in either case the weight of silver is lessened and the value increased.

The third way involves change by adding more copper, and this is the direction that the tricksters are going. Today 20 grains of copper are mixed with 8 ounces of silver; then they go further: Another 20 or 30 grains are mixed in. In this way, a profit of as much as 6 silver pieces on 8 ounces of silver is made because each grain equals in value about 8 *maravedis*. Now if the yearly shipments from the Indies bring in 1,000,000 silver *marks*, at least 500,000 gold coins would be added to the treasury annually by means of this debasing. Furthermore, this income, if sold at 20 percent interest, would annually collect revenue in gold, and the

---

1. When they met on the battlefield in the Trojan war, Glaucus exchanged his gold armor for Diomedes' bronze armor.

profit from this sale would increase to 10,000,000 gold pieces, or, according to the Romans, 4,000 *sesterces*. Once this type of fraud is introduced if more copper is added—as seems likely—profit will increase in direct proportion to the corruption of the metal.

We must recall that silver in Spain for some time has been stamped with the standard of purity of 11 karats (minters call them *dineros*, a standard of silver with 24 grains) and 4 grains, namely, with the admixture of no more that 20 grains of copper. This is established by law for the minters of the kingdom. Silver-smiths follow the same rule in regard to bullion and unworked silver. This is the same silver that they work with in their shops and make into different vessels. The same has been true for many centuries for the old silver in our churches. There is also a law of John II, king of Castile, as promulgated in the 1435 parliament of Madrid (petition 31)—the first law in *novae recopilationis* (bk. 5, title 22). Under these circumstances, I wish to ask these men who want to debase silver: Would their decree apply only to mints, or would it extend also to the workshops of the silversmiths? If they answer, "both places," confusion will certainly reign. The silver already worked will not remain at its previous price. It will also vary in relation to the time when it was made.

Moreover, experts in this field say that silver, debased with more copper, will not be fit for elegant craftsmanship because of its crudity. Should people wish to resist corruption in money and not extend it to silversmiths, they should always bear in mind that silver, both as bullion and as minted, must be of the same quality. Furthermore, silver, as bullion, will always necessarily be worth more than debased money, to the degree that the money has been debased. The complicated process has been going on for a great many years and only the destruction of the robbers and of the entire land will bring it to an end, as Tacitus maintains in a similar instance (*Annals*, bk. 20).[2]

---

2. Tacitus enjoyed an uninterrupted career under the Emperors Vespasian, Titus, and Domitian, which brought him to the praetorship in 88 AD, by which time he was also a member of the prestigious priesthood, the

What, then, is to be done about silver already minted? Is it to be worth the same as new debased money? That would be unjust because the old is better and will contain more silver. Everyone will prefer it to the new, given the choice. However, will it be worth more? That would be fair but also confusing: With the same weight and stamp, some silver coins would be worth more and others, worth less. However, if we wish to go back to an earlier state, and to exchange them for just as many new ones, as we indicated was formerly done in England, that transaction will be just as profitable for the king, as it was in the case of copper money. One must consider, however, if this is a new speculation: to exchange good money for bad. It is not profitable to try people's patience. Patience can become exasperated and wear out and can destroy everything else, as well as be self-destructive.

Now, what will become of gold money? That must be considered too. This issue will certainly confound the highest with the lowest, and turn upside down things better left undisturbed. Once again, the same problems will arise. If gold is not debased, it certainly follows that a gold piece (which we call a *corona*) will not be valued at 12 silver coins but, rather, at 14 or 15, in proportion to the debasing of silver. As silver is debased, commodities always become more expensive. Then foreigners and natives as well, conscious of the situation, will say, "Twelve new silver pieces contain no more silver than 10 of the previous ones; I will subtract the same proportion from the goods I used to

---

college of the *Quindecimviri sacris faciundis*. In 97, he was suffect consul and delivered the funeral oration upon L. Verginius Rufus. We know of no other office held by Tacitus until senority brought him the proconsulship of Asia for 112–13. The date of his death is unknown but is not likely to have been before 118. The *Annals* originally consisted of 18 (or 16) books—6 for Tiberius, 6 for Gaius and Claudius, 6 (or 4) for Nero. Of these there are lost most of 5, all of 7–10, the first half of 11, and everything after the middle of 16. It is not known whether Tacitus completed the *Annals*; nor is the date of composition known with certainty, though scholars seem to think some passages are datable to 114 or 115. (OCD, 1469–71, s.v. Tacitus)

give as well." We explained above what will happen if controls are imposed. Furthermore, not all prices can be controlled. Commerce, when interfered with, is like milk that is so delicate that it is spoiled by the most gentle breeze. As a matter of fact, money—especially silver money, because of its quality—is the ultimate foundation of commerce. When it is altered, everything else resting upon it will necessarily collapse. The stability of silver explains why the disadvantages from the alteration of copper money are not completely obvious. It acts as a restraint on copper money, because, as before, a silver piece is still exchanged for 34 *maravedis* of this new and debased coinage. Without this restraint, commerce would all but fail; everything would cost much more than before.

Moreover, suppose that our only money is copper and that silver is not being transported from the Indies. All the evils described in the previous chapter would suddenly come upon us in one fell swoop. Silver wards off these evils because it is honorable and there is a good supply of it in the country. If this last reason seems weak, then a new and valid argument appears. All monetary income will be diminished to the degree that silver is changed. Someone who has an annuity of 1,000 gold pieces will suddenly receive only 800 or fewer, depending on the degree of debasing of silver. Certainly, when payment is necessarily made in new money, 1,000 gold pieces of new money will not have more silver and will not be more useful for living than 800 previous ones. Therefore, people scarcely coping with previous taxes will be oppressed by a new and very heavy one. Among those affected will be churches, monasteries, hospitals, gentlemen, and orphans—no one will be spared. Earlier, the point was clearly made that a new tax cannot be imposed without the people's consent. We still have to respond to the arguments advanced for the other side. The king gains nothing by profiting at the expense of his subjects, nor may he seize the citizens' possessions by either sheer force, cunning, or deceit. One man's loss is another man's gain. There is no way around that fact.

However, the previous argument asserted that silver was exported because of its excellence. I deny this statement outright, and point out that, although French gold pieces are somewhat better than ours and more valuable, ours are nonetheless found in that country in abundance. Two particular reasons explain this. First, Spaniards import the foreign goods they need and because they cannot exchange an equal amount of their own goods for the imports they have to pay money for the excess. Linen cloth, paper, books, metals, leather goods, trifles, different objects, and, sometimes, grain are imported. Foreigners are under no obligation to give these goods free of charge but they do so for other goods they need and exchange them for money. Second, the king's yearly expenses and payments to foreigners reach 3,000 *sesterces*, seven million a year.[3] Unless this sum were paid out to bankers with the authority to postpone payment, when the king needs it, it would not be at hand. Someone, however, may tenaciously insist that the excellence of silver serves the same purpose. I do not disagree, provided my adversary understands that there is no way to keep foreigners from constantly making their money inferior to ours. In this way, they get their hands on our silver, which they certainly need more than life.

Is there, then, a way to correct the disadvantages that arise from the debasement and abundance of copper money? I have never believed that a concrete disadvantage may be corrected by a greater disadvantage, or a sin by a sin. Some cures are worse than the sickness. Furthermore, I am not aware of any cure for this illness, except the one that our ancestors constantly used in similar straits, namely: The value of the new money is reduced by half or by two-thirds.[4] If that approach is not enough to heal

---

3. The Spanish text reads: "certainly exceed six million." Cf. Juan de Mariana, *Tratado y discurso sobre la moneda de vellón*, ed. L. Beltrán (Madrid: Instituto de Estudios Fiscales, 1987).

4. Recall, by way of illustration, Mariana's earlier examples of John I of Castile (who depreciated the currency by 50 percent) and Henry II of Castile (who depreciated it by 66 percent).

the wound, the bad money is to be completely recalled and good money put in its place. It is, of course, only just that either solution makes the one who profited from the general disaster pay. Because I see this approach is not common—indeed never employed—it is preferable for those who are in possession of the money to suffer a loss. Otherwise, by continuing longer in error, we aggravate the causes of a stubborn illness. On the other hand, we can have recourse to devaluing money. This would involve general disaster for all. It is clear that the pivots on which this entire issue turns are those two values of money that were explained in chapter 4. They must be mutually adjusted if we want things to be sound. That means that money should be legal, but if the values are separated (which, it seems, will happen if silver is debased), every possible evil will come upon the state.

We end with this point: In 1368, when a great part of France was under the English kings,[5] the Prince of Wales,[6] who was

---

5. This is a reference to the Hundred Years' War (1337–1453), which, as described by the *Dictionary of the Middle Ages*, "was actually a series of wars, continuing the succession of Anglo-French conflicts that had begun in 1294. The one significant difference between the wars that preceded 1337 and those that followed was the existence of the Plantagenet claim to the French throne. The English invoked the claim only sporadically, but it enabled them to attract the support of enough anti-Valois magnates to justify the argument that the whole struggle was essentially a civil war between competing factions of French princes. Recent English scholarship permits identification of three twenty-year periods of intense conflict: the Edwardian War of 1340–1360, the Caroline War of 1369–1389, and the Lancastrian War of 1415–1435. The first and third of these were marked by English victories." (DMA, 5, 184, s.v. France: 1314–1494)

6. Edward, Prince of Wales (1330–1376), called the "Black Prince," was the eldest son of Edward III (1312–1377) and Philippa of Hainault. He was created Prince of Wales in 1343. As heir to the English crown, Edward was given honors and symbolic duties from an early age. His involvement with the Hundred Years' War began in 1345 when he led a troupe into France on a burning and pillaging rampage. He gained fame in 1356, at the Battle of Poitiers, where his archers dealt a fatal blow to the French charges. Unskilled as a ruler, however, Edward was never able to master the restless

running affairs in France for his father, the king, levied a new tax on his vassals. He did this because his treasury was exhausted by the wars he was waging on behalf of Peter,[7] the king of Castile. Very many refused to accept this new burden; others like those in Poitiers, Limoges, and La Rochelle agreed, on condition that the prince would not alter money for the next seven years. Jean Froissart,[8] the French historian, relates this in his *Annals* (vol. 1). This account makes it clear that princes have debased money but that the citizenry have always disapproved of and rejected it as they could. It would be beneficial if our people would learn from this example and agree to financial subsidies when the king requests them, on condition that the prince promises that money would be stable for as long as they could demand.

Gascon nobility. "When his Spanish expedition of 1367 led not just to the victory at Navarrete, but also to harse taxation to pay for it, their response was revolt and an appeal to the king of France. Charles V replied on 23 January 1369 by summoning the Black Prince to Paris." In 1370 he lead his last campaign and then returned to England in 1371, where he spent his final years leading the opposition to the Lancastrian party of his brother, John of Gaunt. (DMA, 4, 398–99, s.v. Edward the Black Prince)

7. Mariana is referring to Peter I of Castile and León (1334–1369). For more on Peter, see chapter 6, note 12.

8. Jean Froissart (1337–1410) wrote a four-volume chronicle of England, France, Spain, Portugal, Scotland, Brittany, Flanders, and adjoining countries, which treats extensively the notable events and persons in those countries from 1325–1400. The first volume, which Mariana references in the *Treatise*, covers the period from 1325 to 1378.

12

CONCERNING
GOLD MONEY

Gold money varies greatly. I am not talking about the still extant money of the first Roman Emperors—gold coins minted from the most pure gold with their names inscribed on them. On the other hand, when the Goths were in control in Spain, impure and base gold was coined—gold of 12 or 13 karats—because of many additions. Nonetheless, some of their kings' coins of better gold have been discovered. We have, moreover, seen one coin that was 22 karats. We need not go into the monetary arrangements of the kings of León and Castile when Spain was coming into power: We do not happen to see gold from that period, and it would be very laborious to delay on it.

I will deal only with those changes that were made in gold from the time of King Ferdinand and Queen Isabella. At the beginning of their reign, these rulers minted coins from very pure gold of 23¾ karats, which they called *castellanos*: 50 from 8 ounces of gold, with each coin worth 485 *maravedis*. Thus, the 8 ounces, once minted, were worth 24,250 *maravedis*. However, as bullion of the same quality, the *mark* was worth only 250 *maravedis* less. This difference, after the gold was minted, used to be divided equally among the officers of the mint and the owner of the gold. At the same time, 8 ounces of 22 karat gold bullion was worth 22,000 *maravedis*, and the bullion weight of a *castellano* was worth 440 *maravedis* because gold of that sort was not being minted at that time. Only goldsmiths employed it in their craft. Neighboring nations used gold minted in accordance with our quality and price. This fact created no difficulties.

Then, a little while later, to the glory and prosperity of our nation, the western passage to the Indies was opened and a large amount of gold was imported every year. In their desire for our gold, some of our neighbors debased the quality of their own and others increased the price of ours. Conscious of these ploys, our people did not debase the quality of their gold at that time; they just increased its price. Therefore, in the 1497 parliament of Medina, the same rulers[1] decreed by law that no more *castellanos* were to be minted, but, in their place, *ducats*[2] were to be minted, which they called "excellent." From the previous 8 ounces of gold of the same purity, 65⅓ such coins were to be minted, each valued at 375 *maravedis*. Therefore, minted gold advanced to 24,500 *maravedis*; gold bullion or jewelry of the same weight was worth 24,250 *maravedis*. At the same time, 8 ounces or a *mark* of 22 karat gold was worth 22,500 *maravedis*, and the value of a *castellano* was 450 *maravedis*. This rate continued for several years until it was noticed that the neighbors were further debasing gold.

Thus, in the 1537 parliament of Valladolid, Charles Augustus[3] changed things completely and decreed by law that gold of

1. That is, the Catholic Kings Ferdinand and Isabella of Castile.

2. The Spanish text reads *dineros*. Cf. Juan de Mariana, *Tratado y discurso sobre la moneda de vellón*, ed. L. Beltrán (Madrid: Instituto de Estudios Fiscales, 1987).

3. Charles I of Hapsburg (1500–1558) later became Emperor Charles V of the Holy Roman Empire. As the son of Philip the Handsome, Duke of Burgundy, and Joanna, third child of Ferdinand of Aragón and Isabella of Castile, he was heir presumptive to an empire more vast than

precisely 22 karats was to be minted. Sixty-eight coins were to be minted from 8 ounces, and, called *coronas*, each was worth 350 *maravedis*. As a result, 8 ounces of this money were worth 22,800 *maravedis*. There was no legislation concerning gold bullion or gold, either coined or as jewelry. It was bought and sold by agreement like merchandise. The *novae recopilationis* (bk. 5, pt. 1, law 4, title 24) decrees that goldsmiths were to work no other gold but the purest, or 22 karat, or at least 20 karat. Therefore, unlike silver, gold bullion did not always parallel minted gold and was not governed by the law for minted gold. Nonetheless, for the most part, 22 karat gold was minted and was common with goldsmiths. Because of its lower price in Castile, foreigners kept exporting gold, which had been exchanged for crafts and goods. This fact compelled Philip II, king of Spain, to increase the price of gold in each *corona* by 50 *maravedis* in the parliament of Madrid. Consequently, what used to be valued at 350 *maravedis* went up to 400 *maravedis*. With this law, 8 ounces of

Charlemagne's and over which the "sun never set." The empire included the Netherlands and claims to the Burgundian circle; it included Castile, Aragón, the conquered kingdoms of Navarre and Granada, Naples, Sicily, Sardinia, the conquests of the New World, and possessions in North Africa, all of which after the death of Ferdinand, Charles ruled jointly with his mad mother; it also included the Hapsburg duchies of Austria with rights over Hungary and Bohemia, inherited from his paternal grandfather, Emperor Maximilian I. The main objective of his reign was not new conquest but the protection and consolidation of his inheritance, which he sought to accomplish through strategic matrimonial alliances. As it turns out, his reign would be plagued with international conflict that would eventually overcome him. The conflicts were exacerbated by the Lutheran Reformation in Germany. Shortly before his death, Charles' proposal of the succession of his son Philip to the imperial title was rejected at the Diet of Augsburg and that event, in conjunction with several other blows, led him to abdicate his office. He gave the governments of the Netherlands, Spain, and Sicily to Philip. To Ferdinand, he handed over the Hapsburg Empire, but not the title of Emperor, which he retained until 1558. (NCE, 3, 503–6, s.v. Charles V, Holy Roman Emperor)

minted gold reached 27,200 *maravedis*. The *castellano* was worth 16 silver coins or *reales*.

At this point, we may consider the possibility of debasing gold coins. Just as the quality of copper coins was diminished, and just as they are thinking about doing the same with silver coins—as rumor has it—would the state benefit if the same thing were done with gold coins? They would have less quality and be increased in value. The issue is the same. I personally believe that every alteration in money is very dangerous. It is never expedient to mint unlawful money and thus increase by law the cost of something that is commonly considered to be worth less. Nor can our neighbors be prevented from further debasing their money because of our example. We have learned by experience from the four changes made in gold since the time of the rulers, Ferdinand and Isabella, that it is impossible to prevent the gold from being carried off.

If gold coins are greatly debased, perhaps foreigners would scorn it. Certainly, it would lose much of its value. I doubt that such a situation would befit the majesty of Spain. In my opinion, however, it would not cause serious harm if gold were altered by taking away part of its quality and increasing its price. This is especially true because such a change in the past, when repeated frequently within a few years, did not bring serious disadvantages. The supply of gold is always small in comparison to silver, and its use as money is less common and usual. Therefore, I have not been accustomed to believe that it would be very disadvantageous if an alteration were to occur. In any event, I have always been convinced that I would wish things to hold to their course and not be concerned with money. Nor does the opposite approach benefit in any way, except to provide income for the prince. Income should not always be our goal, especially by this means, that is, debasing money. As a matter of fact, provided that the original quality and reckoning of copper and silver money remain intact, I would not be too concerned about what happens to gold in either way. Two things are important: One, that it be done with the consent of the subjects concerned; the other, that the money always be legitimate or legal and not otherwise. To achieve this end for copper money, both values must be equal: The value of the metal, whether mixed with silver or not, must be computed, as well as the cost of minting. Thus, if 8 ounces, or a *mark*, of copper along with the expenses of minting cost only 80 *maravedis*, it is unreasonable to permit its value to be increased by law to 280 *maravedis*, as is now done. It is unlawful to do so to the degree that legal value deviates from real value. To preserve parity in the case of gold and silver, their proportional relationship must be considered. If they are of equal purity, gold is compared to silver by a ratio of 12 to 1, as Budaeus[4] says in *De asse* (bk. 3). I say of each, "purity or quality," because just as the purity of gold is commonly divided into 24 grades, which the goldsmiths call "karats," so the purity of silver is divided into 12 *dineros*.[5] Thus, silver of 11 *dineros* ably corresponds to 22 karat gold. This proportion generally holds between these two metals. Of course, the ratio would change because of the scarcity or plenitude of one or the other metal. They are like other goods: An ample supply lowers the price, and scarcity raises it. As a result, we should not be surprised that the ancient authors do not agree on how gold and silver were related to one another in value. Therefore, gold and silver money of the same purity and weight should be carefully exchanged at the rate of 12 silver coins for 1 gold coin, as now happens. For that is lawful. If that value is exceeded or lessened, the whole transaction smacks of fraud.

---

4. The French humanist, philosopher, and philologist Guillaume Budé (1468–1540) developed a method of critical-historical analysis of texts. With his work, *De asse et partibus eius Libri quinque* (Paris: Ascensianis, 1514), Budé combined archeology and philology and was, consequently, a founder of the science of numismatics (the study and collection of coins, medals, tokens, paper money, and other human artifacts). Mariana's *De ponderibus et mensuris* displays a similar historical-critical interest in numismatics to Budé's *De asse*.

5. *Dinero* is the standard for silver and is equivalent to 24 grains.

For example, if a gold *corona* is exchanged for 16 or 18 silver ones (*reales*), this transaction is a clear-cut violation of monetary justice, unless, of course, the purity of the gold is increased or the purity of the silver lessened. When such is the case, what seemed to be unjust is lawful and in keeping with equity. Finally, it is of the utmost importance that princes do not profit from debased money. Were that permitted, it would be impossible to curb the greed of foreigners and countrymen who, in the hope of great profit, would force upon us counterfeit and adulterated money of the same kind.

13

IS THERE SOME WAY TO ASSIST THE PRINCE IN HIS NEED?

The popular proverb is quite true: "Necessity knows no law." Another one says: "The stomach has no ears," which is to say that it is a harsh demander; it does not give way to arguments. However, that problem is easily handled. The stomach settles down after eating. Certainly, such needs and wants arise in the state that it is not surprising that those in charge of administration dream up some uncommon and inept remedies. One such remedy is clearly the recently adopted debasement of money. We have explained this point in the arguments of this disputation, but if this remedy is not satisfactory, we will have to find a more suitable way to fill up the treasury.

I do not intend to treat so great an issue. My purpose has been to condemn the alteration of money as a base crime that is full of great disadvantages. It would be pleasant to address some other ways and means—perhaps more suitable and ultimately more fruitful—of enriching the prince. One might add that there are ways and means that involve no injury to, or groaning of the nation; they will, rather, meet with the greatest approval. First, somehow, court expenditures could be lessened, for reasonable and prudent moderation is more splendid and manifests more majesty than unnecessary and unseasonable consumption.

In an account of royal taxes and expenses, receipts, and outlays of John II, king of Castile, for the year 1429, we find that the annual expenses of the court, including the ministers' salaries, gifts, and the royal table, amounted to hardly 30,000 gold pieces. Someone might say that these accounts are very old; everything has changed; prices are much more expensive; kings are more powerful, and, therefore, greater pomp and majesty are found at court. I do not deny these facts, but, really, all of these do not adequately explain the difference between the 30,000 of those days and the 120,000 that are spent at this time for the support of the court. Moreover, a more recent account of royal taxes, with the expenses for 1564 for the court of Philip II king of Spain, for the support of prince Charles his son,[1] and for John of Austria,[2] reports that annually they amounted to no more than 40,000 gold pieces.

---

1. Don Carlos (1545–1568), the Infante of Spain, was born of Philip's first wife Maria of Portugal who died in childbirth. His second marriage to Mary Tudor was barren and devoid of love. His third marriage to Elizabeth of Valois was a diplomatic arrangement. Philip grew to love her and was heartbroken when she died in 1568, having borne him two surviving daughters. Elizabeth's death was preceded that same year by the death of Don Carlos, Philip's infirm son who was mentally and physically handicapped. Given Don Carlos' condition, Philip regarded him as permanently unfit to rule and so put him into confinement in January 1568. In 1579, Philip married his fourth and final wife, Anne of Austria, who bore five children but only one of which survived and who later succeeded his father as Philip III. (NCE, 11, 273, s.v. Philip II, King of Spain)

2. Don Juan of Austria (1547–1578), the natural born son of Emperor Charles V and Barbara Blomberg and half-brother to Philip II of Spain, is remembered for leading the Christian fleet to victory at the Battle of Lepanto, an engagement fought between the Christian and Turkish fleets on October 7, 1571, and the last great naval battle under oars. (NCE, 8, 665–66, s.v. Lepanto, Battle of)

How, you ask, can court expenses be curtailed? I do not know. Prudent men who are involved in the court should make that determination. Common opinion has it that whatever the purveyor hands over to the stewards is stored in the pantry and paid for automatically. Second, royal gifts would perhaps be smaller if a large tax were added to them. I do not believe that a king should have a reputation for being cheap, or not be sufficiently generous in response to his people's good works and services. I believe that two things have to be taken into consideration. There is, of course, no nation in the world with more and greater public rewards available: commissions, offices, pensions, benefices, military towns, and gifts. Were these distributed reasonably and deliberately, one could dispense with extraordinary gifts from the royal treasury and other income. In addition, we should remember that excessive gifts do not make men more disposed for service, or even well disposed to the giver. It is human to be led on more by the hope of a future reward than by the memory of a favor received. This is so true that those who have prospered much at court constantly think of retirement and the peaceful life.

No king of Castile lived more magnificently than did Henry IV, and in no other time was the unrest as great. As a result, after Henry's abdication, the nobles made his brother, Alfonso,[3] king.

---

3. Alfonso XII of Castile (?–1468) succeeded to the throne in 1465 after a revolt (of the nobility) the previous year deposed his brother Henry IV. Henry was forced to recognize his brother Alfonso as heir to the throne over his own daughter Juana. After Alfonso's death in 1467, the nobles turned to Henry's half-sister Isabella. "The princess, however, was of different mettle, and she disregarded the advances of the nobility. In the pact of Los Toros de Guisando (1468), Henry recognized Isabella as his successor as long as she was willing to accept his guidance on the selection of her husband. Their peaceful relations only lasted a short time. The next year Isabella married Ferdinand of Aragón, prince and heir of the neighboring kingdom, without her brother's consent. When Henry recognized his daughter Juana … as his heir (1470), civil war broke out. After Henry's death in 1474, Isabella, with the support of the Castilian bourgeoisie and of her husband, was proclaimed queen of Castile." (DMA, 3, 138, s.v. Castile)

After his death, they offered the kingdom to Isabella, who was the sister of both of them. Tacitus makes a telling comment at the end of book 19[4]: "Vitellius,[5] inasmuch as he wished to have friends because of the greatness of his gifts rather than because of the constancy of his morals, bought more friends than he had." Robert of Sorbonne,[6] his confessor and Archdeacon of Tornai,

---

4. This sentence is found at the conclusion of book 3 of his *Histories*. See *The Complete Works of Tacitus*, trans. A. J. Church and W. J. Brodribb, ed. Moses Hadas (New York: The Modern Library, 1942), 3.86, p. 591: "Believing that friendship may be retained by munificent gifts rather than by consistency of character, he deserved more of it than he secured."

5. Vittelius (15–69 AD) was a Roman emperor who met a tragic fate. Already a consul in 48, he became proconsul of Africa then served as legate to his brother in the same post. Galba appointed him governor of Lower Germany in November 68, perhaps thinking that his reputed indolence made him less of a political threat. Vittelius won over the disaffected soldiers in the province by an ostentatious display of generosity. On January 2, 69, Vittelius was proclaimed emperor by his troops and quickly won the support of the legions of Upper Germany, which had refused allegiance to Galba the day before. After consolidating his support, he marched on Rome in July, made offerings to Nero, and had himself created consul in perpetuity. However, he did nothing to appease troops that had been defeated in earlier battles. In July, Vespasian became emperor and soon marched with troops from the east to invade Italy. Vittelius failed to block the Alpine passes and suffered defeat. Vespasian's forces attacked Rome and overcome Vittelius' resistance. On December 20, 69, Vittelius was dragged through the streets, humiliated, tortured, and killed. (OCD, 1608–9, s.v. Vittelius, Aulus)

6. Robert de Sorbon (1201–1274) was a theologian and founder of the Sorbonne, the first endowed college of the University of Paris. He became a master theologian (*c.* 1236) and as master regent taught at the University of Paris from 1254–1274. Robert was a contemporary and colleague of Thomas Aquinas, Bonaventure, Albert the Great, and Giles of Rome. Named chaplain of Cambrai (*c.* 1250) and in 1258 at Notre Dame de Paris, he belonged to the circle of friends of Louis IX who regarded him as a man of great wisdom and chose him as his confessor. His renown stems from the initiative he took to found a college for "poor lay theology students." His project won the interest of Louis IX, the bishops, and even the pope, and he opened the college in October 1257. After a well-organized search

tells us in his life of Saint Louis,[7] king of France, that when he wanted to establish a college in Paris that still bears his name, the Sorbonne—no other college in the world may be compared with it for learning—he asked the king for a contribution. The king answered that he would willingly comply with his request if only chosen theologians, after examining public expenses and income, would determine how he might lawfully contribute to this work. He was a great king and a real saint. If he did not lavish money on this holy work without discernment and examination, would he squander it on fattening up the courtiers on the vain pleasures of gardens and unnecessary buildings? The reality is that a king has income from the nation to support public works. When he has taken care of them, he may direct it to other things—but not before. If I were to send a commissioner to Rome to foster my affairs, would he be permitted to divert the money that I gave him for necessary expenses to other uses?

A king is not permitted to apply money given to him by his subjects as freely as he may apply income from lands held as a private citizen. Furthermore, he should exempt himself from unnecessary expenditures and from wars. Parts that cannot be cured should be timely cut off from the rest of the body. Philip II, king of Spain, wisely separated the Belgians from the rest of

---

for suitable property, he bought almost all the houses in the neighborhood of Rue Coupe Gueule, a site still occupied by the Sorbonne. He gave the institution carefully planned statutes that provided for the recruitment, common life, and studies of the students who took up residence there. Mariana studied for five years (1569–1574) at the Sorbonne. (NCE, 13, 440, s.v. Sorbon, Robert de)

7. Louis IX of France (1214–1270) succeeded to the throne in 1226. He married Marguerite of Provence in 1234, and they had ten children together. He is best remembered for his crusades and for the way he promoted peace and justice throughout his long reign. He drew up new ordinances to improve public administration, to eradicate corruption, and to improve the law of his dominions. (NCE, 8, 1010–12, s.v. Louis IX, King of France, St.)

his empire.[8] Mapheius[9] indicates in *Indicarum historiarum* (bk. 6) that the Chinese nation—an empire once much bigger than it is now—as if in a bloodletting and correction of excess, gave up many lands that it could not conveniently govern. Emperor Hadrian[10] did the same thing when he destroyed the bridge that Trajan had built over the Danube. He wished the Danube on the north and the Euphrates in the East to be the limits of the Roman empire, which was already struggling under its own weight.

The fourth rule should be that, first of all, court ministers must be accountable and after them the magistrates of the provinces and all others who play any role in the state. We are in a dangerous situation where hardly anyone is safe. The way that people think is pitiful. They believe that merit now has nothing to do with gaining anything in our land: office, commission, benefice, and even a bishopric. Everything is for sale, and nothing is conferred without its price. Although it may not be true and is exaggerated, it is pernicious to have such a thing stated.

---

8. The forfeiture of the northern provinces of the Netherlands occurred in 1581.

9. The Jesuit Giovanni P. Maffei (1536–1603) wrote an "Indian History" (that is, a history of eastern peoples) in Latin. The original title was *Historiarum Indicarum libri XVI* (Florence, 1588). As a professor of rhetoric, he was educated in Latin, Greek, and Hebrew; his literary style was thought to be highly refined and, consequently, was emulated widely by later Jesuit writers.

10. Hadrian (76–138 AD) was adopted emperor in 117. His goal as emperor was to establish natural or manmade boundaries for the empire. He realized that the empire's extent had severely strained its capacity to maintain and protect itself. Consolidation, not expansion, was his policy, and this brought him trouble in the early years, when Trajan's (53–117 AD) eastern conquests were abandoned. Hadrian's own military experience was extensive. He had served in provinces in the east, along the Danube, and along the Rhine. Soon after his arrival in Rome, he began several lengthy journeys that took him to nearly every province. He spent more than half his reign traveling abroad. (OCD, 662–63, s.v. Hadrian [Publius Aelius Hadrianus])

In general, royal ministers and penniless nobodies enter upon public commissions and almost instantly become blessed and reckon their annuities in thousands of gold pieces. All these things come from the blood of the poor, from the very marrow of litigants and office-seekers. Moreover, such transformations have led me to think that the state would benefit if it adopted the ways of the Church. Before they assume office, bishops must present a witnessed account of all their possessions. Then, at death, they may leave these things, and nothing else, to those whom they wish. The chosen ministers of court, or magistrates, or other commissioners should have to do what bishops do. Through periodic investigations, they will be forced to render an account of their newly acquired wealth and will be stripped of that wealth whose definite sources and causes they fail to identify. The treasury would greatly profit from money recovered should this inquiry and investigation be instituted.

Public opinion often condemns those in charge of royal taxes because, by agreement with tax collectors, they usurp a sizable part of the gain and money that the collectors gather. Worse yet, in every city, leaders make money by selling the local or royal laws every year to those who refuse to obey them. They openly grant public privileges to those from whom they secretly receive money. We cannot ignore the different forms of corruption and ways of cheating the provincials. When King Philip II recently decreed that the value of *coronados* rise by an eighth, a favorite of the king with knowledge of this decision was proven to have scraped together all the gold brought across the Atlantic each year and to have made a huge profit.

A certain Jewish chief treasurer asked one of the earlier kings of Castile—John II or his father Henry[11] I believe—why he did not play dice with his courtiers to pass the time. The king answered, "How can I do that since I do not own a hundred gold pieces?" The treasurer let that pass at the time. Later, at an opportune

---

11. That is, Henry III of Castile (1390–1406).

moment, he said, "O King, your statement to me the other day sorely disturbed me. So much so, that I thought I was being indirectly rebuked. If you agree, I will make you wealthy and happy instead of poor." The king went with his proposal. Then, the treasurer said, "I want control of three secluded castles." There he intended to keep money and the prisoners proved guilty of crimes in the use of royal money. Then, questioning minor treasurers, he kept finding the royal name on forged documents and other bequests of the prince, paid with a third or a fourth subtracted for those who handled the royal promissory notes. Then he asked those who had been defrauded if they would be content with half of what they had lost and if they would give the rest to the king. They agreed, considering the offer a gain, since until then they had no hope of future compensation. When these arrangements had been made, he put the treasurer and his bailsmen into chains, where they remained until payment of all the money. In this way, he enriched the treasury.

It would be nice if such could occur now. It would save a large amount of money. Nowadays, this new corruption is an indication of the perverted government—treasurers purchase their positions at a large price—and have to sell the office and profit from the misery of others. They invest the royal money in commerce and do not meet royal debts for a year or two. Most conveniently, after four or eight months they pay the debt, even with some expense deducted, namely, an ounce or two ounces from the entire sum as they agreed with the creditor. Such corruption could be eradicated if individuals were investigated as we mentioned above. Truly or falsely, the claim is commonly made that every one of these treasurers has supporters in the court among the magistrates. Part of the explanation for this is, of course, the hope for peculation, and this misfortune is no less deadly than the earlier ones. Above all, the royal taxes and income should be taken care of diligently and faithfully. Under current practice, scarcely half of the taxes and income is turned to royal use. Money, transferred through many ministers, is like a liquid. It always leaves a residue in the container. Our *Annals*[12] (bk. 19, chap. 14) testify that the king of Castile, Henry III, by exercising such care, escaped the shameless poverty once found in his court. He used to have to buy ram's meat for dinner and finally wound up very wealthy. He left his son, John II, huge treasures without any complaints from the provincials. His only warning to him and to his brother Ferdinand[13] was not to let the ministers get their greedy hands on public money.

Finally, strange and luxurious merchandise—which softens people and that we can do without and suffer no harm—should be sold at a high tariff, for such an approach will discourage their import, which is something very desirable. On the other hand, if they are imported, the treasury will be bolstered by the tariff levied upon delicacies of foreign people: gold brocade, tapestries, all sorts of perfumes, sugar, and delicacies. Alexander Severus[14] did this once in Rome and was endlessly praised. We have discussed this point rather fully in our *De rege et regis institutione*[15] (bk. 3, chap. 7), and there is no need to dwell on

---

12. Juan de Mariana, *Historiae de rebus Hispaniae* (Toledo: Thomae Gusmanii, 1595). This title is Mariana's first main work.

13. Ferdinand I of Aragón (1380–1416), also known as Ferdinand of Antequera, was chosen in 1412 by electors of parliaments in the penisular realms to assume the Aragonese throne. Ferdinand was related both to Peter IV of Aragón and the king of Castile. James of Urgell, the other contender, rebelled but was captured in 1413 and died in prison twenty years later. The election of Ferdinand was a fateful turning point for Aragón, "the dynastic ratification of Castile's demographic and military superiority. Ferdinand and his sons ruling after him were Castilians who married Castilians and appointed Castilians, and they were in real and constant danger of losing touch with their subjects." (DMA, 1, 417, s.v. Aragón, Crown of (1137–1479)

14. Marcus Aurelius Severus Alexander (209–235 AD), son of Iulia Avita Mamaea by her second husband, the procurator Gessius Marcianus of Arca Caesarea in Syria, was adopted emperor in 222. (OCD, 222, s.v. Aurelius Severus Alexander, Marcus)

15. Juan de Mariana, *De rege et regis institutione libri III* (Toledo: Petrum Rodericum, 1599). This title is Mariana's second main work.

it here. I add only this point: The ways to provide for the royal needs discussed here, indeed any one of them, would provide more than the 200,000 gold pieces annually, which is the same amount the first authors promised the king in their paper on debasing copper money. Moreover, this will happen without any censure from the people. Rather, the poor will enthusiastically support the measure.

There might be an objection that we should not be surprised to find a means—that is, debasing coinage, being employed that different kings used in the past. We readily reply. Times have changed much since the past: The king's income was much less then; there was no sales tax; there was no gold from the Indies; there was no tax on wine and oil; there were no monopolies, no Church tithes, no crusade subsidies; and kings were not grand masters of military orders. Every year, all of these provide abundant income. The problems were greater at that time: The Moors were at the gates, there were wars with neighboring kings, the nobles were frequently in revolt, and internal rebellion resulted. Now, on the other hand, by the grace of God there is internal peace throughout all of Spain. I will say absolutely nothing about foreign affairs. In 1540, Francis I,[16] king of France, debased the *solidus*—the nation's common coin—and his son Henry[17] mixed

---

16. For more on Francis I, see chapter 2, note 3.

17. Henry II of France (1519–1559) succeeded to the throne in 1547. He was the second son of Francis I and Claude. When only seven years old he was sent by his father, with his brother the dauphin Francis, as a hostage to Spain in 1526; after peace was reached at Cambrai in 1530 they both returned home. In 1533, he was wed to Catherine de' Medici. In 1536, Henry, formerly duke of Orleans, became Dauphin by the death of his older brother Francis. From that time forward he was strongly influenced by two persons: Diane of Poitiers, his mistress, and Anne de Montmorency, his mentor. His younger brother, Charles of Orleans, was his father's favorite. Henry supported the constable Montmorency when he was disgraced in 1541, protested against the treaty of Crépy in 1544, and at the end of his reign held himself aloof. His accession in 1547 created quite a stir at court. Henry was a robust man but had weak character and mediocre intelligence.

in even more copper. Charles IX,[18] following the example of his grandfather and his father, reduced its quality and weight even further. Great difficulties were certainly impending, but the monetary troubles were so great that there was no need to lament the other evils. The afflicted people were in tumult: Ancient religious convictions were changed at random and very many, driven by want, changed their countries and lived at the mercy of others.

The account in our *Annals* (bk. 29, chap. 12) deserves mention here. Because of Philip of Austria's death and the weakness of his bereaved wife, Maximilian Augustus,[19] and Ferdinand the Catholic were long at odds over the administration of Castile and were considering some means of reaching peace. Among other things, Augustus was demanding the payment of 100,000 gold pieces from the income of Castile. The Catholic king was not able to grant the request and pleaded as an excuse that the public debt had increased to 500,000 gold pieces. Clearly, this is

---

He was cold, haughty, melancholy, and dull. During his reign, the royal authority became more severe and absolute than ever. He showed no mercy to Protestants. He was injured in a jousting accident and died several days later. (EB, 13, 291, s.v. Henry II, King of France)

18. Charles IX of France (1550–1574) succeeded to the throne in 1560. He was the third son of Henry II and Catherine de' Medici. He was first known as the duke of Orleans until the death of his brother Francis II in 1560, at which time he became king. Still a minor, the power was in the hands of the queen-mother, Catherine. Charles' weaknesses were his passionate nature and his imaginative pursuits. Hunting, violent exercise, and poetry were his undoing. He submitted easily to his mother's authority, which freed him to pursue his own interests. In 1570, he was wed to Elizabeth of Austria, daughter of Maximilian II. After the massacre of Saint Bartholomew, in which he displayed a weak and intemperate character, he became melancholy, severe, and taciturn. (EB, 5, 921, s.v. Charles IX, King of France)

19. Maximilian I (1459–1519), "the last knight," German emperor from 1493 on, married his son Philip of Austria (i.e., Philip the Handsome) to Joanna the Mad, the daughter (third child) of Ferdinand and Isabella of Castile. (EtR, 4, 77, s.v. Maximilian I)

a remarkable response. Taxes were much less than they are now, wars were more serious than ever, and corresponding hopes were aroused. Portugal was conquered and driven out of our territory; Atlantic trade was open; the kingdom of Granada was subjugated; the coasts of Africa, the Basques, and Neapolitans were defeated; moreover, there was peace in the kingdom, and the Italian wars in which the kingdom always played a major role were abating. Nevertheless, the kingdom was oppressed by a burden that was indeed light if compared with the debts of our day. It makes sense. A prince of outstanding prudence kept account of income and outlays and did not wish to be pressed further. That is great wisdom. It is not reasonable to blame the times. That incident took place in 1509 when a good deal of gold was being brought into the treasury every year. I do not believe that times have changed since then, but men, abilities, morals, and pleasures have changed. The weight of these evils will dash this empire to the ground if God does not support it with his favor and saving hand.

Such are my thoughts on the subjects discussed in this disputation and particularly on the subject of altering and debasing copper money. If such is done, without consulting the people, it is unjust; if done with their consent, it is in many ways fatal. If my arguments have been true and reasonable, I thank God. If, however, I have been mistaken, I certainly deserve to be pardoned because of my sincere desire to help. My knowledge of past evils makes me afraid that we will fall into misfortunes from which it will be difficult to extricate ourselves, but if my statements in this disputation have irritated anyone, he should recall that salubrious remedies are frequently bitter and stinging. Moreover, when a subject is a common concern, everyone is free to express his opinion on it, whether he speaks the truth or is mistaken. Finally, I beg God to shed his light upon the eyes and minds of those who are responsible for these things so that they may peacefully agree to embrace and put into action wholesome advice once it is known.

About the
Contributors

Jordan J. Ballor is a research fellow at the Acton Institute
for the Study of Religion & Liberty, as well as a doctor desig-
natus in Reformation history at the University of Zurich and
a doctoral candidate in moral and historical theology at Cal-
vin Theological Seminary. Jordan serves as executive editor of
the *Journal of Markets & Morality*, a peer-reviewed academic
journal promoting intellectual exploration of the relationship
between economics and morality from both social science and
theological perspectives.

Patrick T. Brannan, SJ, has the AB/MA (Cantab.) in the Classical Tripos from Cambridge University in England and the PhD
in Classical Philology from Stanford University in California, as
well as the ecclesiastical degrees PhL and STL in philosophy and
theology. He has taught classical languages and some philosophy
and theology (mainly in seminaries) and has done a good deal
of translation. In Rome he was a translator at the Thirty-Fourth
General Congregation of the Society of Jesus and also attended
two Synods of Bishops in the Vatican as a translator of documents in French, German, Italian, Latin, Spanish, and English.

ALEJANDRO A. CHAFUEN is president of the Atlas Economic Research Foundation. He is the author of *Faith and Liberty: The Economic Thought of the Late Scholastics* (Lexington, 2003) and *Economia y Etica: Raices Cristianas de la Economia Libre de Mercado* (RIALP, 1991), as well as numerous articles in economics, economic history, and the philosophy of economics. He is an active member of the Mont Pelerin Society and the Philadelphia Society.

STEPHEN J. GRABILL serves as senior research scholar in theology and director of programs at the Acton Institute for the Study of Religion & Liberty. He is editor emeritus of the *Journal of Markets & Morality*, as well as author of *Rediscovering the Natural Law in Reformed Theological Ethics* (Eerdmans, 2006) and editor of *Sourcebook in Late-Scholastic Monetary Theory* (Lexington, 2007).

Christian's ▞▞LIBRARY PRESS

Founded in 1979 by Gerard Berghoef and Lester DeKoster, CHRISTIAN'S LIBRARY PRESS has been committed to publishing influential texts on church leadership, the vocation of work, and stewardship for more than thirty years. During that time Berghoef and DeKoster wrote significant works including *The Deacons Handbook*, *The Elders Handbook*, and *God's Yardstick*, which still are in demand today. After the passing of Lester DeKoster in 2009, the imprint is now administered by the Acton Institute for the Study of Religion & Liberty. For more information about Christian's Library Press, visit www.clpress.com.

ACTON INSTITUTE

With its commitment to pursue a society that is free and virtuous, the ACTON INSTITUTE FOR THE STUDY OF RELIGION & LIBERTY is a leading voice in the international environmental and social policy debate. With offices in Grand Rapids, Michigan, and Rome, Italy, as well as affiliates in four other nations around the world, the Acton Institute is uniquely positioned to comment on the sound economic and moral foundations necessary to sustain humane environmental and social policies. The Acton Institute is a nonprofit, ecumenical think tank working internationally to "promote a free and virtuous society characterized by individual liberty and sustained by religious principles." For more on the Acton Institute, please visit www.acton.org.

Made in the USA
Charleston, SC
29 May 2013